THE COMPLETE HISTORY OF
AVIATION
FROM BALLOONING TO SUPERSONIC FLIGHT

TRANSPORTATION AND SOCIETY

THE COMPLETE HISTORY OF

AVIATION

FROM BALLOONING TO SUPERSONIC FLIGHT

EDITED BY ROBERT CURLEY , MANAGER, SCIENCE AND TECHNOLOGY

Educational Publishing

IN ASSOCIATION WITH

EDUCATIONAL SERVICES

Published in 2012 by Britannica Educational Publishing
(a trademark of Encyclopædia Britannica, Inc.)
in association with Rosen Educational Services, LLC
29 East 21st Street, New York, NY 10010.

Distributed exclusively by Rosen Educational Services.
For a listing of additional Britannica Educational Publishing titles, call toll free (800) 237-9932.

First Edition

Britannica Educational Publishing
Michael I. Levy: Executive Editor
J.E. Luebering: Senior Manager
Marilyn L. Barton: Senior Coordinator, Production Control
Steven Bosco: Director, Editorial Technologies
Lisa S. Braucher: Senior Producer and Data Editor
Yvette Charboneau: Senior Copy Editor
Kathy Nakamura: Manager, Media Acquisition
Robert Curley: Manager, Science and Technology

Rosen Educational Services
Jeanne Nagle: Senior Editor
Nelson Sá: Art Director
Cindy Reiman: Photography Manager
Karen Huang: Photo Researcher
Brian Garvey: Designer
Matt Cauli: Cover Design
Introduction by Laura Loria

Library of Congress Cataloging-in-Publication Data

The complete history of aviation: from ballooning to supersonic flight/edited by Robert
Curley.—1st ed.
    p. cm.—(Transportation and society)
"In association with Britannica Educational Publishing, Rosen Educational Services."
Includes bibliographical references and index.
ISBN 978-1-61530-667-1 (library binding)
1. Aeronautics—Juvenile literature. I. Curley, Robert, 1955–
TL547.C575 2012
629.13009—dc23
                                                              2011018093

Manufactured in the United States of America

On the cover: *A jet fighter plane soars above the clouds. Jet-engine fighter planes were used sparingly during World War II, and were refined in the post-war years.* Shutterstock.com

On page viii: *Hot air balloons take flight near Canterbury, Eng., as part of a mass crossing of the English Channel on April 7, 2011.* Oli Scarff/Getty Images

Pages 1, 18, 36, 52, 82, 104, 123, 145, 156, 158, 161 Shutterstock.com

66

95

96

INTRODUCTION

A little more than a century ago, Wilbur and Orville Wright achieved the first powered, sustained, and controlled flight of an airplane, an experiment that changed the world. However, the principles of flight were established well before then, studied and tested by explorers and inventors worldwide. From the ancient Greek inventor Archimedes to the Wright brothers and beyond, humankind has sought to unlock the secrets of flight, finding a way for humans to defy gravity and slip the bonds that keep us earthbound. *The History of Flight* examines the origins of this quest, explains the mechanisms by which flight is possible, and tells the story of how aviation has evolved.

The earliest forays into human flight were in balloons. Balloon flight is possible because of buoyancy, which allows a balloon to carry a weight that is less than or equal to the difference between the weight of the balloon (and its enclosed gas) and that of the air that it displaces. A balloon's buoyancy can be controlled by changing the amount of gas in the envelope (in the case of a gas balloon) or by changing the temperature of the air within the envelope (in the case of a hot-air balloon), thereby changing its weight relative to the amount of air it displaces. In addition to an envelope and a heat source, hot-air balloons designed for travel have a basket, or gondola, for the passengers and instruments, and an air-release system for controlled descent and landing.

The Montgolfier brothers of late 18th-century France were the fathers of hot-air ballooning. In a smallish balloon of their own creation—with an envelope of cloth and paper enclosing air heated by burning straw—they made the first successful unmanned balloon flight in June of 1783. In November of that year, fellow Frenchmen Jean-François Pilâtre de Rozier and François Laurent, marquis d'Arlandes achieved a 10-mile manned flight over Paris, witnessed by France's King Louis XVI and American inventor and statesman Benjamin Franklin.

Over the next two centuries, fuel sources for hot-air balloons moved from the Montgolfiers' original burning straw to include coal gas, petroleum, and propane. Envelope design evolved as well, moving from cloth and paper to include silk and nylon, and, in the case of superpressure balloons, polyester. Propane burners and nylon or polyester envelopes remain popular in hot-air ballooning today.

Ballooning in the 20th century pushed the boundaries of the craft. The development of pressurized suits and cabins allowed for high-altitude flight. High-altitude balloons have specific practical applications, for example, aerial photography and cosmic ray research. Modern-day adventurers pushed the limits of ballooning, including Steve Fossett, who made the first solo balloon flight around the world in 2002. Ballooning also has become a popular leisure activity. Commercial hot-air balloons can carry as many as 20 passengers.

Flight via airships enjoyed a brief popularity in the first decades of the 20th century. There are three types of airships. Non-rigid airships, commonly called "blimps," are made of material similar to that used for the envelopes of gas balloons. Rather than a basket, however, an airship envelope is attached to a car that has rudders and a set of propellers driven by engines. Semi-rigid airships also are similar to blimps but have a metal keel running the length of the balloon's base.

Finally, rigid airships are made of a fabric envelope supported on a frame of metal. This type of aircraft saw some success as a means of transport in the 1920s and '30s. Dirigibles designed by (and named after) Ferdinand von Zeppelin were used for military purposes during

World War I by both Germany and the Allies. The famous *Hindenburg*—the largest dirigible ever constructed—made a series of cross-Atlantic passenger trips in the 1930s, culminating in a spectacular crash on May 6, 1937, in New Jersey. The ship ignited and burned upon landing, killing 36 of its 97 occupants.

Dirigibles became obsolete not only because of their limitations and safety concerns, but also due to the advancements in heavier-than-air craft, or airplanes. At the dawn of the 20th century, three obstacles to airplane flight remained—lift, propulsion, and control. The solution to the first problem, lift, lay in the design of wings for the aircraft. The earliest aircraft wing designs mimicked the flapping motion of birds. In the early 1880s, Englishman George Cayley designed an aircraft wing patterned after the shape, rather than the motion, of a bird's wing, which led to the creation of the first cambered, or arched, airplane wing. German mechanical engineer Otto Lilienthal compiled data on Cayley's design, which led him to build and successfully fly a number of gliders. The Wright brothers used Lilienthal's data in their plane designs.

The next obstacle was propulsion. Until the late 19th century, machines with adequate power to propel an aircraft were too heavy. By the end of the century, however, internal-combustion engines had solved this problem. The Wright flyer of 1903, Orville and Wilbur's first plane, had a lightweight 12-horsepower, four-cylinder engine designed by the Wright brothers' machinist, Charles Taylor.

Regarding the matter of control—the last problem to be solved—a successful flight system had to take into account full control over the balance and steering of the airplane in all three dimensions: roll (the banking of the plane), pitch (the direction of the nose up or down), and yaw (the direction of the nose to right or left). The Wrights' solution included "wing-warping," or changing the angle of the wings to control the plane's roll, an elevator to control pitch, and a rudder to control yaw. In 1903, having surmounted the roadblocks to construction of a controllable flying machine, the Wright brothers debuted their plane at Kill Devil Hills, near Kitty Hawk in North Carolina. The age of airplane travel had begun.

Europe eagerly embraced airplane research and development in the years leading up to World War I. During the war, investors began to explore the nonmilitary applications of planes as a means of travel. Surplus military planes were employed for passenger travel and mail delivery in the postwar years. Competition, both commercial and personal, led to longer flights, across continents and oceans, with European and American aviators trying to best duration and speed records through the 1920s and '30s. Government-subsidized airlines were founded in Britain and France; operations in the Netherlands, Germany, and the Soviet Union weren't far behind.

Meanwhile, in the United States, decommissioned military planes were at first used primarily for airmail service. The United States encouraged private development of its airplane industry, and the competition among private entrepreneurs ultimately improved the design and safety of planes. Boeing and the Douglas Aircraft Company, with its DC line, were dominant players in the burgeoning U.S. airplane industry.

With the arrival of passenger air travel came the need for regulation and safety standards. In the United States, a number of organizations were created to investigate airplane accidents and determine their causes.

In the 1920s, a private organization called the Daniel Guggenheim Fund for the Promotion of Aeronautics conducted experiments with instrumentation and "blind flight," supported advances in the meteorological sciences, and established university programs in aeronautical engineering.

World War II temporarily stalled the private air industry, as airplanes were appropriated for military use. The United States provided nearly all of the planes for the Allies during the war, due mainly to the reliability of planes such as the DC-3, as well as the country's ability to meet production quotas. The U.S. Army Air Force Air Transport Command (ATC) created airfields, communication centres, and weather forecasting stations around the world. Using the ATC as a model, the International Civil Aviation Organization (ICAO) was founded after the war, in 1947. An arm of the United Nations, the ICAO standardized aviation terminology, safety procedures, and equipment, and established English as the universal language for global flights.

Airlines flourished after the war. Flying became the premiere mode of travel, with airlines booking more passengers than railways and ships by the 1950s. Due to an uptick in business, fares were lowered and flights became an affordable means of transportation for the average citizen. The use of aircraft for personal, business, and "utility" (surveying, crop dusting, etc.) purposes also increased. Together, all modes of air transportation not connected to military or scheduled airline flights were referenced under the term "general aviation."

As piston engines reached the limits of their performance, airplane designers turned to jet engines, which were simpler in design, longer-lasting, and more efficient at high altitudes. Jet engines had been around since the late 1930's but came into common usage by the 1950s. The switch to jet engines necessitated changes to the design of airplanes. Airlines restocked their fleets with jet planes such as the American DC-8 and the French Caravelle. Jet technology proved expensive, so booking more passengers was required to make it economically feasible for the airlines to make the switch. Other aviation changes and improvements during the "jet age" included the addition of the "black box" data recorders and satellite navigation.

Other means of air travel were developed or refined in the 20th century, including hang gliders and ultralight airplanes. There also were aircraft that operated using vertical lift. The gyroplane was first successfully launched in 1907 by the Brequet brothers in France. It only rose two feet off of the ground and was tethered due to its lack of control, but it was successful enough to serve as something of a prototype. From there two distinct machines were created—the autogiro and the helicopter.

Using motor-driven horizontal rotors, helicopters could take off vertically, thus eliminating the need for runways. However, these machines required a more developed structure and finely tuned control than a plane. By 1941, the first modern helicopter had appeared, complete with a three-blade main rotor for lift and a small vertical tail rotor to counteract torque. The development of controls—collective pitch, throttle, antitorque, and cyclic-pitch—allowed for smooth liftoffs, flights, and landings. Modern helicopters also feature retractable landing gear, navigational equipment, and instruments similar to those in airplanes.

Before World War II, planes only needed runways of about 2,000 feet—and those were rarely paved. Airports were located near city centres and frequently near water as well, for seaplane landings. Today's 100 or so large hub airports around the world are vast operations, with extensive space dedicated to paved runways and operational facilities. More than half of these larger airports are located in the United States.

The operations of an airport have two basic divisions — the airside and the landside. Airside facilities include the runways and plane taxi areas, air traffic control and navigation, emergency services, and maintenance. Landside facilities include the passenger terminal, cargo areas, and access roads. Airports are often managed by independent agencies licensed by the government, although many of the services within are provided by other agencies, public and private. When selecting a site for a new airport, location and the airport's effect on surrounding areas are carefully considered. Accessibility, noise, and terrain are some of the factors that determine airport placement.

In response to a number of hijackings and other terrorist threats to commercial aircraft during the 1960s and '70s, the International Civil Aviation Organization issued several recommendations aimed at air travel. However, compliance with the ICAO measures varied. Essentially the only solid standards were that passenger belongings were screened, and the public was denied access to certain areas. Since the attacks of September 11, 2001, however, airport design and operation have undergone major changes. Scrutiny of passengers and their belongings has intensified, creating a massive expansion of security personnel and equipment, and necessitating that passengers arrive well ahead of scheduled flights to allow enough time for screening. Additional attention has been paid to locating parking and loading areas outside of the airport, to reduce the damage caused by vehicular explosions.

Human life has been irrevocably altered since the advent of flight. Before airplane travel was common, an individual who moved far from home might never have returned. Mail sent long distances could take weeks to arrive. Nations at war could wait as long as a month for supplies and troops to arrive. Air travel has made our world more accessible, and thus more interdependent. *The History of Flight* details the fascinating journey that has brought the nations and peoples of the world closer together.

CHAPTER 1

BALLOON FLIGHT

The first untethered manned balloon ascent took place on Nov. 21, 1783, when two Frenchmen climbed into a wicker basket suspended from the base of a beautifully decorated, paper-lined cotton balloon. The balloon, filled with air heated by burning straw, carried the men aloft for a little more than 20 minutes over Paris. Witnessing this ascension were Louis XVI, members of the French Academy of Sciences, and multitudes of the public, including the American inventor and statesman Benjamin Franklin. This event left a profound impression on the world of the 18th century: Men had actually flown!

Since that time, the field of flight has been taken over by airships, gliders, airplanes, helicopters, and even rockets and spacecraft, but balloons continue to be used for recreation, competitive sport, and scientific exploration. Hot-air balloons may be used for short flights at low altitudes or taken on "long jumps," using stronger winter winds to travel hundreds of kilometres at altitudes of up to about 3 km (2 miles). Gas balloons can stay aloft for several days and travel a thousand kilometres or more. Indeed, combination hot-air and gas balloons have crossed continents and oceans and even circled the globe. For scientific research, special gas balloons can float in stable conditions for days or even months at a time, carrying instrument payloads through the upper reaches of the stratosphere.

ELEMENTS OF BALLOON FLIGHT

Technically speaking, balloon flight (or "lighter-than-air flight") is the passage through the air of a balloon that contains a buoyant gas such as helium or heated air. The three basic principles of buoyancy were discovered by the ancient Greek mathematician and inventor Archimedes, the 17th-century British natural philosopher Robert Boyle, and the 18th-century French physicist Jacques-Alexandre-César Charles:

1. Archimedes' principle (3rd century BCE), which states that any body completely or partially submerged in a fluid (gas or liquid) at rest is acted upon by an upward, or buoyant, force the magnitude of which is equal to the weight of the fluid displaced by the body;
2. Boyle's law (1662), which states that the pressure of a given quantity of gas varies inversely as its volume at constant temperature; and
3. Charles's law (1787), which states that the volume occupied by a fixed amount of gas is directly proportional to its absolute temperature, if the pressure remains constant.

A balloon can carry the difference between its weight (including its enclosed gas) and the weight of the air that it displaces. Nine cubic metres (1,000 cubic feet) of hydrogen weighs about 2.2 kg (5 pounds), the same volume of helium weighs about 4.5 kg (10 pounds), methane 18 kg (40 pounds), and hot air, at normal hot-air balloon operating temperatures, 22.5 kg (50 pounds). Thus, the lifting force of a chosen gas at low altitudes can be obtained by subtracting its weight from the typical weight of the same volume of air (about 34 kg, or 75 pounds, in this example).

Because the atmosphere is compressed by its own weight, it is less dense at higher altitudes. At 3,600 metres (about 12,000 feet) the atmosphere is approximately two-thirds as dense and so will provide two-thirds the buoyancy. This effect continues progressively, so that at 15,000 metres (50,000 feet) it is only one-tenth as dense, at 30,000 metres (100,000 feet) one-hundredth, and at 45,000 metres (150,000 feet) one-thousandth. In order to carry the same load at an altitude of 50 km (30 miles) as at sea level, a balloon would have to be 1,000 times as big and yet weigh the same (that is, keeping everything constant except the balloon's volume).

The buoyancy of a hot-air balloon is controlled by heating the air in the balloon or by changing the amount of ballast (extra weight). The buoyancy of a gas balloon is controlled by changing the amount of gas in the balloon or the amount of ballast. Tiny changes in one of these components can force dramatic changes in a balloon's flight. Just a one- or two-degree change in temperature in a hot-air balloon, a few grams of ballast dropped, or a tiny release of gas will make a balloon ascend or descend accordingly. On the other hand, in violent maneuvers (such as during a storm), whole bags of sand or great blasts of heat from a balloon's burner may be required for a proper correction. To help in rapid atmospheric cooling, modern hot-air balloons also have very large hot-air release vents in the form of a parachute that can seal and unseal an opening in the top of the balloon.

Changing the altitude of a balloon will permit it to follow different air currents. A 20- or 30-degree difference in wind direction usually occurs in the first few thousand metres of altitude, but a full circle of wind directions ("box winds") can also occur. Albuquerque, N.M., is famous for its box winds, which can be used to climb and descend back to the original launch site. If there is only a simple and stable wind pattern, no additional control is possible. With superior weather monitoring, use of the global positioning system (GPS), and radio or satellite communication, remarkable flight control is now possible. This element of control, or the lack of it, is the hallmark of sport ballooning.

The Fédération Aéronautique Internationale was founded in France in 1905. This nongovernmental organization maintains records for manned flights from balloons to spacecraft, as well as records for flights of model aircraft, unmanned aerial vehicles, and sporting events. In addition, various national aeronautics organizations, such as the Balloon Federation of America and the British Balloon and Airship Club, maintain ballooning records. Airworthiness and operating criteria are controlled in the United States by the Federal Aviation Administration (FAA). FAA regulations for ballooning are generally used by all countries, with only minor local variations.

THE PIONEERS

Credit for the invention of ballooning goes to a pair of 18th-century brothers, Joseph-Michel and Jacques-Étienne Montgolfier of Annonay, a small town just south of Lyon, France. The Italian-born English scientist Tiberius Cavallo had recently demonstrated that Archimedes' principle is applicable to airborne objects by successfully floating hydrogen-filled soap bubbles. When he attempted to duplicate this with animal bladders, though, they proved too heavy to ascend. Fortunately, the provincial Montgolfiers were not constrained by laboratory techniques and created their hot-air balloon on a cruder and much larger scale. Because the area (and therefore the weight) of a balloon goes up by the square of its diameter and the volume (and therefore the lift) increases by the

THE MONTGOLFIER BROTHERS

Joseph-Michel Montgolfier (1740–1810) and Jacques-Étienne Montgolfier (1745–99) were 2 of 16 children of Pierre Montgolfier, whose prosperous paper factories in the small town of Vidalon, near Annonay, in southern France, ensured the financial support of the two brothers' balloon experiments. In 1782 they discovered that heated air, when collected inside a large lightweight paper or fabric bag, caused the bag to rise into the air. (According to one story, possibly apocryphal, the brothers took inspiration from watching Joseph's wife's skirts as they billowed in the kitchen from the heat of a charcoal burner being used to dry laundry.) The Montgolfiers made the first public demonstration of this discovery on June 4, 1783, at the marketplace in Annonay. They filled their balloon with heated air by burning straw and wool under the opening at the bottom of the bag. The balloon rose into the air about 1,000 metres (3,000 feet), remained there some 10 minutes, and then settled to the ground more than 2 km (1.5 mile) from where it rose.

The Montgolfiers traveled to Paris and then to Versailles, where they repeated the experiment with a larger balloon on Sept. 19, 1783, sending a sheep, a rooster, and a duck aloft as passengers. The balloon floated for about 8 minutes and landed safely about 3 km (2 miles) from the launch site. On Nov. 21, 1783, the first manned untethered flight took place in a Montgolfier balloon with Jean-François Pilâtre de Rozier and François Laurent, marquis d'Arlandes, as passengers. The balloon sailed over Paris, traveling 9 km (5.5 miles) in about 25 minutes.

The two brothers were honoured by the French Académie des Sciences for their invention. They published books on aeronautics and continued their scientific careers. Joseph also invented a calorimeter and the hydraulic ram, and Étienne developed a process for manufacturing vellum. In later years, modifications and improvements of their basic design for hot-air balloons were incorporated in the construction of larger balloons that opened the way to exploration of the upper atmosphere. For this reason the Montgolfier brothers are considered to be the first pioneers of balloon flight.

cube of its diameter, they succeeded handily. On June 4, 1783, they made a public demonstration in Annonay with a 10.5-metre (35-foot) diameter unmanned cloth-and-paper balloon, using the heat from a straw fire.

With the news from Annonay, French inventor Jacques-Alexandre-César Charles, who knew that hydrogen was lighter than the hot-air smoke used by the Montgolfiers, realized that all he had to do to succeed was to make his balloon experiment on a larger scale. The first space race was on. On Aug. 27, 1783, Charles launched an unmanned varnished-silk hydrogen balloon from Paris. It was attacked and destroyed by local villagers when it landed near Gonesse some 15 km (9 miles) to the northeast. The Montgolfiers countered by launching a hot-air balloon carrying a sheep, a duck, and a rooster from Versailles on September 19 to determine if the animals could survive in the open air at higher altitudes. The first person at the landing site of the

French aeronauts Jacques-Alexandre-César Charles and Marie-Noël Robert made the first manned ascent in a gas balloon, Dec. 1, 1783. © Photos.com/ Jupiterimages

menagerie balloon was Jean-François Pilâtre de Rozier, who would become the first balloon pilot.

While Charles was designing—and having engineering brothers Marie-Noël and Anne-Jean Robert build—a larger hydrogen balloon that could carry him aloft, de Rozier was teaching himself to fly a hot-air balloon by first going up with a restraining rope. Before Charles could get his gas balloon ready, de Rozier and François Laurent, marquis d'Arlandes, persuaded the king to permit them to make the first manned free flight. On November 21 they went aloft over Paris. A little more than 20 minutes and 16 km (10 miles) later, they safely returned to Earth. Ten days later Charles made the first manned gas balloon ascension, accompanied by Marie-Noël Robert. On landing near Nesles, some 36 km (22 miles) away from

Jean-François Pilâtre de Rozier and François Laurent, marquis d'Arlandes, ascending in a Montgolfier balloon at the Château de la Muette, Paris, Nov. 21, 1783. © Photos.com/Jupiterimages

the launch in Paris, Robert stepped out to let Charles make a second flight. The balloon ascended at a terrifying rate with Charles on the world's first solo free flight. The balloon finally leveled out at about 3,000 metres (10,000 feet), and he was able to bring it down safely.

Most of the features of the classic free balloon were included in Charles's first machine. Important later additions were the rip panel, first used on April 27, 1839, by the American aeronaut John Wise, and the drag rope, invented about 1830 by the English aeronaut Charles Green. A rip panel is an elongated section of the balloon that is lightly fixed in place and can be quickly ripped or pulled open at the moment of landing. It adds greatly to the safety of ballooning by making quick deflation possible. The drag rope, or compensator, serves two purposes. It is a long, heavy rope that trails the balloon in order to slow down the balloon's vertical and horizontal speed in landing operations before the basket touches down. If a landing is aborted, the rope is automatically recovered and can be used again. In areas without electrical power lines, balloons can "drag rope" for many kilometres at a time without having to drop sand or release gas.

THE GAS-HOT-AIR HYBRID BALLOON

Within two years of his epoch-making first manned free flight, de Rozier began thinking about flying across the English Channel. To compensate for the shortcomings of the two types of balloons—hot-air and hydrogen—he combined a hydrogen envelope with a small hot-air envelope below it. Hydrogen provided the basic lift, while the hot-air balloon system allowed him to control his flight without having to constantly drop ballast or release gas. His balloon, christened *Tour de Calais*, was brilliantly decorated with artwork and metallic gilding. According to modern investigations, the metallic coating caused a static discharge that ignited the varnished envelope some 30 minutes after its launch from Boulogne on June 15, 1785. De Rozier and his passenger, Pierre-Jules Romain, died within minutes of the ensuing crash, becoming the first balloon fatalities. Despite this tragic failure, de Rozier's invention eventually succeeded in the ultimate transglobal balloon voyage two centuries later.

The three basic types of balloons (hot air, gas, and a gas-hot-air hybrid) were, then, all invented at the very beginning. A fourth type, the superpressure balloon, which is kept at a constant volume, was proposed by French Gen. Jean Meusnier on Dec. 3, 1783, but not successfully built until stronger materials became available in the 1950s.

SMOKE AND COAL GAS

Smoke balloons, without onboard fire, became popular for fairs and exhibitions as parachutes were perfected. In particular, the standard grand climax of many celebrations at the turn of the 20th century was to have a trapeze artist ascend for hundreds of metres below a balloon belching black smoke before jumping from the trapeze to parachute back to Earth.

The smoke was not just for dramatic effect; it was essential to retain heat, as no fire was carried onboard. Clean air cools rapidly in an ascending balloon, not only by radiation but also by the adiabatic process of expansion. The heat in the carbon particles of smoke, however, is not affected by the change in atmospheric pressure during an ascent, so the smoke acts as a heat sink in addition to freshly sealing the porous muslin fabric that was typically used in such balloons.

On July 19, 1821, at the coronation in London of George IV, Charles Green made the first ascent in a balloon

Illustration showing typical performances by aerial balloonists. Prints and Photographs Division/Library of Congress, Washington, D.C. (digital. id. cph 3g10308)

inflated with coal gas. He also made a historic flight on Nov. 7, 1836, from London to Weilburg, Duchy of Nassau (now in Germany), a distance of about 800 km (500 miles). Other great flights of the period included French aeronaut François Arban's September 1849 flight across the Alps and John Wise's 1,300-km (800-mile) flight from St. Louis, Mo., to Henderson, N.Y. Wise's flight, which was launched on July 1, 1859, was a test of the air currents for a proposed transatlantic attempt.

MILITARY EXPERIMENTS AND PETROLEUM FUEL

Manned balloons have had only minimal military use, the Siege of Paris (Sept. 19, 1870–Jan. 28, 1871), during the Franco-Prussian War being a notable exception. Mail, carrier pigeons, and important individuals were transported in balloons built in the unused Paris railway stations, and the pigeons brought mail back.

In 1903 the Rev. John M. Bacon invented the forerunner of the modern hot-air balloon in England. While coal gas was plentiful and inexpensive locally, expeditionary forces had severe logistic problems with producing hydrogen in the field or transporting heavy compressed-gas cylinders. Bacon promoted the concept of performing military observations with a hot-air balloon that would burn petroleum. His trials in the summer of 1903 were successful, but he did not pursue it further and his work went unnoticed in the ballooning community.

During the 1930s, attempts were made to utilize petroleum or propane fuels by German and Austrian pioneers. Their efforts were technically promising, but they did not replace the sport gas balloon. The philosophy of ballooning entailed long flights at considerable altitude. Hydrogen

French republican politician Léon Gambetta (in hat, centre) about to escape besieged Paris for Tours by balloon, October 1870, during the Franco-Prussian War. © Photos.com/Jupiterimages

and coal gas were plentiful, inexpensive, and accepted fearlessly. Heavy cotton balloons with their cumbersome fuel systems were not suited to traditional ballooning routines. Even in England, where long-duration gas flights were not possible for fear of the sea, there was no interest.

BALLOONS REACH THE STRATOSPHERE

Unmanned sounding balloons for high-altitude scientific investigations were introduced in 1893, but manned ballooning was limited to moderate altitudes until the 1930s. In 1931 Swiss physicist Auguste Piccard inverted a 1905 conception devised by him and his twin brother, Jean Piccard, for a diving ship (bathyscaphe). The 1931 invention consisted of a spherical aluminum pressure cabin and a 14,000-cubic-metre (500,000-cubic-foot) lightweight rubberized-cotton netless hydrogen balloon. This would make possible the first successful stratosphere flight. It carried Auguste and his assistant, Paul Kipfer, to 15,781 metres (51,775 feet) on May 27, 1931. Jean Piccard and his wife, Jeannette, went to 17,550 metres (57,579 feet) on Oct. 23, 1934, with a slightly larger duplicate that used a magnesium-alloy cabin. The official project was completed earlier when U.S. Navy Lieut. Comdr. Thomas G. W. Settle achieved a world-record flight of 18,665 metres (61,237 feet) in the same balloon on Nov. 20, 1933.

Jean and Jeannette Piccard's balloon had several novel advances, the most significant being the remote-control pyrotechnic ballasting system. Contrary to conventional designs, they used blasting caps and trinitrotoluene (TNT) to cut cords outside the sealed capsule.

The Piccard 17,550-metre flight was followed by long-time *National Geographic* magazine contributor Capt. A. Stevens and Capt. Orville Anderson, both of the U.S. Army Air Corps, going to 22,065 metres (72,395 feet) on Nov. 11, 1935. The flight was sponsored by the National Geographic Society and the U.S. Army Air Corps. Stevens and Anderson used a 100,000-cubic-metre (3,700,000-cubic-foot) rubberized-cotton balloon carrying a large magnesium-alloy cabin. That balloon, the *Explorer II*, was seven times the size of Piccard's, but still with very similar fabric. The stress in the skin of the giant balloon was formidable, resulting in repeated failures. On one occasion the crew, this time including Maj. William E. Kepner, barely escaped by parachute.

PLASTIC BALLOONS

Jean Piccard realized that the giant single-cell balloon had reached the end of its practical development. Larger balloons would require heavier fabric with diminishing returns. Small latex balloons were routinely carrying light loads to much greater heights, and Piccard postulated that with a cluster of these he could extend the limits of ballooning. Thomas H. Johnson of the Franklin Institute suggested using fewer but larger cellophane balloons. Piccard, working with Johnson, designed a netless film balloon that substituted a conical skin section for the suspension system. The payload was attached directly to the base of the cone. By 1937 Piccard and his students at the University of Minnesota, including Robert Gilruth (later head of Project Mercury), had flown one of these unmanned balloons about 1,000 km (600 miles), carrying an automatic ballast-releasing device and radio instrumentation.

Piccard dreamed of a stratosphere flight with a cluster of film balloons, but there was concern that they would become tangled. To test the concept, he made a successful solo flight in the *Pleiades* with an ensemble of 92 latex balloons on July 18, 1937.

After World War II, General Mills, Inc., accepted a contract from the U.S. Office of Naval Research to advance the theory of ballooning. The DuPont Company's new polyethylene film was chosen for the envelope. Launches of individual test balloons were finally successful, but there was little faith that the complicated task of rigging 80 of these at once would work, and the project was abandoned. However, the plastic balloon had been created, and they constantly grew larger and more acceptable as polyethylene films improved.

The conversion of the seam tapes—from their original simple joining task to backup use over heat-welded seams and, finally, with reinforcing filaments, to the primary structural load-bearing factor—enabled further size increases and advanced reliability. Their use also enabled the abandonment of the load ring in the mouth of the balloon. This facilitated the development of the natural shape.

In December 1955 the U.S. Air Force established Project Man High to obtain scientific data on the stratosphere and to test equipment for exploring above Earth's atmosphere. Three pilots, Capt. Joseph W. Kittinger, Maj. David Simmons, and Lieut. Clifton M. McClure, in *Manhigh I* (June 2, 1957), *Manhigh II* (Aug. 19, 1957), and *Manhigh III* (Oct. 8, 1958), respectively, each ascended to about 30 km (19 miles) aboard a single-cell plastic balloon. Unmanned flights, generally carrying scientific research payloads of more than 2,250 kg (5,000 pounds), have reached altitudes above 42 km (26 miles) with balloons as big as 1,000,000 cubic metres (some 40,000,000 cubic feet).

SUPERPRESSURE BALLOONS

Polyester film at a tensile strength of 1,400 kg per square cm (20,000 pounds per square inch)—compared with polyethylene at a tensile strength of about 40 kg per square cm (600 pounds per square inch)—finally made it possible to produce superpressure balloons, which do not expand or contract as the enclosed gas heats up or cools down.

A series of contracts were awarded to the G.T. Schjeldahl Company by the U.S. Air Force in the late 1950s to develop polyester balloons. After repeated failures, Donald Piccard (son of Jean and Jeannette Piccard) was assigned the project. He theorized that the failures were caused by the self-destructive tendencies of the stiff film. By laminating two layers of very thin Mylar, he produced a more flexible film that resulted in the first successful superpressure balloon. These balloons have been used by

A weather balloon is released at a weather station at the South Pole. NOAA

the U.S. National Center for Atmospheric Research to carry instrumentation aloft for months at a time, continually circumnavigating Earth.

Manned superpressure balloons have had some success but have not yet been able to carry on through diurnal heating cycles.

MODERN HOT-AIR BALLOONS

A small group of engineers under Wes Borgeson at General Mills developed a polyethylene hot-air balloon with a propane burner that was successfully flown by Tom Olson and later by Paul ("Ed") Yost perhaps as early as 1955. Yost, then at Raven Industries, made the first publicized flight of the modern hot-air balloon in 1961 at Bruning, Neb. The balloon, developed for "silent entry" (military) use, was soon found to be unsuited for covert operations because of the noise and light from the burners, and the classified project was apparently abandoned. Although these balloons proved unsuitable for military use, Mark Semich and Donald Piccard pursued their American manufacture for sport service.

Yost's hot-air balloon, using strong and durable nylon fabric instead of gossamer polyethylene, did not use load tapes. While load tapes had been an important factor in the success of film balloons, they were considered unnecessary for fabric balloons. However, with the growth of sport ballooning, a longer life and a safer design were required. In 1964 Donald Piccard adopted the full-length load tapes found on plastic balloons for fabric balloons. Coincidentally, this afforded the opportunity for his invention of the bulbous gore, or pumpkin-shaped balloon.

American aeronaut Tracy Barnes adapted a venting system used in parachutes to make the most important advance in safety and control of hot-air balloons since the rip panel. Barnes's parachute top has also been used in gas balloons. His novel three-corner basket and three-point suspension distinguish his balloons from the commonplace.

CHAPTER 2
FLIGHT BALLOONS
AND AIRSHIPS

L ighter-than-air flight is performed most often by hot-air balloons, which use gas burners to heat the air enclosed in a fabric envelope. In addition, gas balloons are used for high-altitude ballooning, usually for scientific research purposes, and long-distance flights have been achieved by hot-air balloons, gas balloons, and combination hot-air and gas balloons. Airships are a type of lighter-than-air craft that enjoyed a brief ascendancy in the early 20th century and are seen today in only small numbers.

HOT-AIR BALLOONING

Hot-air balloons are commonly used for recreational purposes. In addition to quiet morning or afternoon flights drifting cross-country to enjoy the view, many balloonists enjoy competitive sporting events and attempting to set new records. A balloonist may fly alone in the basket or carry several passengers. Often several balloons meet to launch together without any competitive goals. Individual flights generally last from one to three hours and may go several kilometres, though they often land very close to the take-off point.

Balloon rallies may consist of just a few balloons for a one-day outing or up to several hundred balloons for a weeklong festival. Competitive events include distance within a time limit, spot landing, and "hare and hound" races. Hare and hound races are easy to organize and judge since they require only one (hare) balloon to launch first and fly a reasonable distance. The competitors attempt to land as close as possible to the hare's landing position. In crowded conditions, markers are often dropped to simulate the landings, and the balloons fly on to more open locations.

Commercial ride operators are in business almost everywhere in the world. Some ride balloons carry 10 to 20 passengers at a time in gigantic partitioned baskets. In California and France, wine-country flights are popular tourist attractions. African safari flights, at low altitude over vast game preserves, are perhaps the pinnacle of ride ballooning.

HOT-AIR BALLOON COMPONENTS

Hot-air balloons consist of the balloon envelope, which contains the heated air that gives the craft its buoyancy; the system of burners that heats the air contained by the envelope; and some sort of basket or gondola to carry pilots, passengers, and supplies.

ENVELOPE DESIGN

Hot-air balloons vary considerably in design and materials. Lightweight coated nylon and polyester fabrics are the most common materials for envelopes. Cotton is very serviceable but has a comparatively poor weight-to-strength ratio and is only favoured for carnival "smoke" balloons. Specially shaped balloons, which are literally pneumatic sculptures, are popular at public events. They utilize special tailoring and many internal baffles and cords to attain the desired designs.

Sport balloons typically have a silhouette similar to the natural shape of fully inflated gas balloons. They can

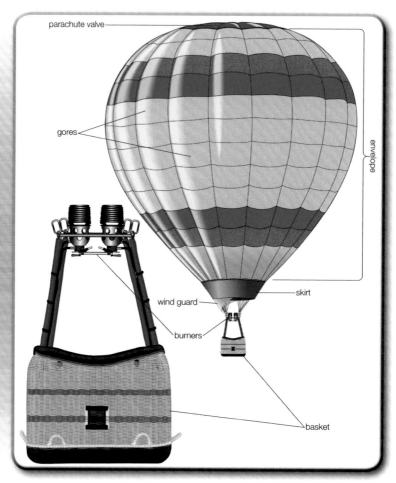

parachute valve

gores

envelope

skirt

wind guard

burners

basket

Basic components of a hot-air balloon. Encyclopædia Britannica, Inc.

be assembled with many vertical gores (fabric sections, or panels) or fewer horizontal gores. The gore material can be cut straight (with the fabric's natural grain) or on the bias (diagonal to the fabric's natural grain). If straight gores are used, excess material can be gathered to create a fluted pattern that provides some flexibility. Gores made of bias-cut materials have greater stretch, which provides a natural flexibility. With horizontal gores, the individual panels can be gathered to provide a bulbous gore, which gives even greater flexibility. Because of the greatly reduced effective radius of curvature, a bulbous gore balloon experiences much less stress on the envelope fabric.

With bias gores, load tapes known as tensors are generally sewn loosely into ducts formed in the vertical seams, much like the shroud lines sewn into a parachute's radial seams. With other balloons, the load is carried in tapes sewn or heat-sealed directly to the vertical seams. One load tape can and should have more than enough strength to carry the whole load without an excessive weight penalty. The stress in the skin of the balloon is so low that normal handling will cause visible damage if the fabric is weakened by wear or exposure long before it would fail in normal flight. The importance of load tapes and adequate excess strength in them in balloon construction cannot be overemphasized. Catastrophic failure in a properly designed balloon is extremely rare.

DEFLATION SYSTEMS

Landing a bag with some four tons of air in it at 30 km (20 miles) per hour without wheels, steering gear, or brakes presents some problems. Prior to John Wise's discovery of the rip panel deflation system in the mid-19th century, a gas balloon could be dragged along for several kilometres before coming to a stop. In particular, balloons on extended flights seemed to be drawn into low pressure systems, which often resulted in stormy landings.

The basic hot-air balloon rip panel is a simple large sleeve at the apex that is drawn into a bunch and tied off with a cord. The cord is typically cut remotely by an electrically actuated explosive squib cannon or released with a pull cord moments before touchdown in order to deflate the envelope rapidly. This configuration is known as a pop top. Other balloon models use a circular panel held in place with a hook-and-loop (e.g., Velcro) closure that can be opened and closed progressively for finer adjustments in buoyancy. That system is more often replaced with Tracy Barnes's "parachute top," which is a combination venting and deflation panel. The parachute top consists of a simple hole at the apex of the balloon, usually about one-quarter of the balloon's diameter, plugged with a parachute of slightly greater diameter. The parachute is positioned by cords radiating out a few metres from the parachute's edge to anchors located on the puffy gore centres. A venting cord leads from the juncture of the parachute's shroud lines to the basket. Sometimes a mechanical advantage is gained by a pulley system. Pulling the cord draws the parachute down into the balloon, thereby letting hot air escape. Releasing the cord snaps the parachute back into the closed position with the force of the hot air. If the parachute is pulled far enough into the balloon, it will collapse, letting the balloon completely deflate rapidly. This is a great advantage in high-wind landings, where it might be difficult to maintain tension on the cord. Some versions use separate retracting cords to force the opening to close, redundant cinch cords to bunch the parachute for hands-off deflation, and elastic centring cords to provide automatic rapid setting and resetting of the parachute.

BURNERS

Early hot-air balloons burned straw and alcohol spirits for fuel, though by 1900 these fuels had been replaced with petroleum. Compressed liquefied propane is used almost exclusively today. Hot-air balloon burners use vaporizing coils to preheat the fuel for efficient combustion. Most of these coils are made of stainless steel, but copper coils also work adequately. The burners are mounted, often on gimbals, on the suspension concentration ring between the basket and the mouth of the balloon. A secondary system without vaporization and slower air mixing can provide much quieter operation and give redundancy for safety. Many designs use multiple duplicate burners and fuel supplies because there has been a history of leaking seals on control valves and occasionally contaminated fuel.

BASKETS

Passenger baskets, or gondolas, vary as much in design as envelopes. For easy transportation, collapsible tubular frames with stout fabric covers can meet minimum requirements. Originally, wicker baskets had manila rope woven into the basket for suspension, but because of the potential for rot, these were replaced with synthetic or steel cables. Heavy wickerwork frames, using rattan up to a few centimetres in diameter, typically have also been replaced with metal or plastic framing.

Wicker construction has an advantage over metal skeletons and hard fibreglass shells in its absorption of the kinetic energy of impacts, however. Wicker is also favoured for its nostalgic artistic appearance. Any basket can have closed-cell foam padding on the inside for passenger safety and comfort.

Metallic components present hazards in the event of contact with electrical power lines. However, wickerwork by itself provides little protection to the passengers or fuel tanks from such contact. Vacuum-formed monocoque plastic baskets are slowly coming into use. They provide advanced impact and electrical contact resistance.

HIGH-ALTITUDE BALLOONING

Since the 18th century, ballooning has continually achieved higher altitudes. From Charles's 3,000-metre

(10,000-foot) ascent in 1783 to U.S. Army Air Corps Capt. Hawthorne C. Gray's fatal ascent to 12,950 metres (42,470 feet) in 1927, the maximum altitude was only limited by the pilot's need for oxygen. Lacking confidence in the ability to seal an aircraft hermetically, American aviation pioneer Wiley Post and others concentrated on individual pressure suits. Even as late as 1937, prominent aeronautical engineers publicly derided the concept of building airplane pressure cabins.

The Piccard invention of the stratosphere balloon opened up new heights for exploration. The first stratosphere flights were mounted to study cosmic rays, which are absorbed as they enter Earth's atmosphere. Early high-altitude work with plastic balloons continued cosmic ray research, air sampling for detecting atomic explosions, photographic flights over foreign terrain, astronomical observations above the disturbances of the troposphere, and even aerodynamic testing of free-falling payloads. A balloon is the only stable platform for any type of observation above the range of airplanes and below the range of orbital spacecraft. It is also the only aircraft that does not affect its environment and the only device that can sit relatively motionless above heights obtainable by helicopters.

Balloons for high-altitude research are generally made of polyethylene or polyester film. Some of these polyethylene films are less than a tenth of a millimetre thick. In order to carry a payload, the seams are reinforced with load-bearing tape. When a scientific payload is attached to the bottom point of a modern balloon, the envelope, if given overall excess material circumferentially, will form the shape of an acorn squash. This is a result of the natural stresses on the "skin" caused by the tension from the payload and the varying internal forces of the gas, which depend on the elevation inside the balloon. Additional excess material in the horizontal dimension will only result in loose wrinkles. Less horizontal fullness will cause tight spots or even indentations. A large lightly loaded balloon will be very "fat." The top will have a large flat or even indented area, and the bottom point will have an obtuse included angle. If the balloon envelope is only a small percentage of the total weight, the balloon will have more of an inverted teardrop shape, and the bottom point will have an acute included angle. This family of cross sections is known as the "natural shape."

High-altitude plastic balloons are only partially inflated at launch to allow for gas expansion as the balloon climbs. This expansion is roughly tenfold for each 15,000 metres (50,000 feet) of altitude. In flight the payload is generally suspended from an open extended parachute connected at its apex to the base of the balloon. The parachute can be released by radio control. At the moment of release, the elasticity of the parachute snaps it open almost instantly. A radio-controlled gas valve can be used at the top of the balloon. Excess gas is vented by ducts high on the side of the balloon, with their openings at the base level. If the duct is placed high enough on the balloon, it is impossible for outside air to enter the balloon.

Contamination of the lifting gas by outside air will lower the possible ceiling of the balloon and, in the case of hydrogen, create a fire hazard. The design must assure that flow resistance in the duct does not create adverse back pressure, which would burst the balloon. The diameter of the duct, its length, and any possible kinks must be considered. The weight of the duct itself can pull it down enough to block the opening into the balloon in some cases. With the duct design, any entrained air from mishandling during inflation or minute leaks in the balloon below the base of the lifting gas will pool in the base of the balloon and lower the ceiling accordingly.

A high-altitude research balloon preparing for takeoff at NASA's Goddard Space Flight Center in Maryland. The inverted teardrop shape of the balloon indicates that the envelope accounts for a small percentage of the total weight of the craft. SSPL via Getty Images

The natural shape gives a balloon very low skin stress under static conditions. At altitude the balloon is very stable and not generally subject to turbulence or dynamic loads. On the way up, the balloon is only partially inflated and has great flexibility to distort, relieving any stress.

The first manned stratosphere balloon used a spherical aluminum cabin. Following ones used magnesium alloys and spun aluminum. Current high-altitude pressure cabins are made with various composite materials. Internal pressure is maintained by onboard liquid oxygen supplies and air scrubbers to remove carbon dioxide, moisture, and other body products.

Several flights have been made with no cabin at all. Crews in open gondolas wear space suits similar to those that astronauts wear.

LONG-DISTANCE BALLOONING

Flying for ever greater distances has always been a goal of balloonists. The first successful aerial crossing of the English Channel occurred on Jan. 7, 1785, in a gas balloon piloted by French balloonist Jean-Pierre Blanchard and American balloonist John Jeffries. Another early long-distance flight was by the English balloonist Charles Green, accompanied by the Irish musician Thomas ("Monck") Mason, aboard the *Great Balloon of Nassau* in November 1836. Taking off from London, they traveled about 750 km (480 miles) in 18 hours to land in the Duchy of Nassau (now in Germany). Paul ("Ed") Yost and Donald Piccard made the first hot-air balloon crossing of the English Channel in 1963.

The New York Sun newspaper reported on April 13, 1844, that Monck Mason had made the first transatlantic balloon crossing, but the report turned out to be a hoax perpetrated by Edgar Allan Poe. The actual first transatlantic balloon crossing occurred in 1978 aboard the *Double Eagle II*, a helium-filled balloon built by Yost, with piloting duties shared by three New Mexico businessmen, Ben L. Abruzzo, Maxie Anderson, and Larry M. Newman. The first transpacific balloon flight was made in 1981 by Americans Abruzzo, Newman, Ron Clark, and Rocky Aoki aboard the helium-filled *Double Eagle V*.

In 1987 British entrepreneur Richard Branson and Swedish aeronaut Per Lindstrand, aboard the *Virgin Atlantic Flyer*, made the first transatlantic flight in a hot-air balloon. And in 1991, aboard the *Otsuka Flyer*, they made the first transpacific flight in a hot-air balloon. In 1984 American aviator Joseph W. Kittinger, aboard the helium-filled *Rosie O'Grady's Balloon of Peace*, made the first solo transatlantic balloon flight. In 1995 American adventurer Steve Fossett, aboard the helium-filled *Solo Challenger*, made the first solo transpacific balloon flight.

Several around-the-world balloon flights were attempted with various systems, but success was finally achieved in 1999 by Swiss balloonist Bertrand Piccard (son of Jacques Piccard, grandson of Auguste Piccard, and second cousin of Donald Piccard) and British balloonist Brian Jones aboard a combination hot-air and helium balloon, the *Breitling Orbiter III*, with a pressurized cabin. The first solo around-the-world balloon flight was made by Fossett aboard a combination helium and hot-air balloon, the *Bud Light Spirit of Freedom*, in 2002.

The success of the *Breitling* and *Spirit of Freedom* depended on several independent factors. Balloon design, cabin design, and meteorological technique were all unique and individually critical. While it may be possible to use other techniques, all manned major long-distance efforts have utilized the jet stream. This limits the altitude, track, and season for a successful attempt to the winter months

Richard Branson (left, front) *sitting in the cabin of the* Virgin Atlantic Flyer *prior to making the first transatlantic flight in a hot-air balloon.* Hulton Archive/Getty Images

in mid-latitudes at elevations of about 6,000 to 10,000 metres (about 20,000 to 35,000 feet).

In order to navigate a balloon on a long-distance flight, the pilot must take advantage of meteorological conditions. Sensitive attention to altitude, rate of climb, and global positioning instrumentation is essential in order to follow minute-by-minute advice from ground-based weather coaches. Information, including complete weather maps, can be communicated by wireless Internet e-mail connections. For an intercontinental flight, which may take several days, reevaluation of computer-generated weather predictions is important; for global circumnavigation it is essential.

For a successful global voyage only a general meteorological condition can be chosen. It is impossible to calculate weather conditions two and three weeks in advance at locations around the world. The general

STEVE FOSSETT CIRCLES THE GLOBE

James Stephen Fossett was born on April 22, 1944, in Jackson, Tenn. He grew up in California, where he studied economics and philosophy at Stanford University (B.A., 1966). After earning an M.B.A. (1968) at Washington University in St. Louis, Mo., he became a successful commodities broker, and in 1980 he founded the securities company Lakota Trading.

Fossett undertook a number of challenges, including swimming the English Channel (1985), before gaining international attention with his ballooning feats. In 1995 he registered his first record in the sport with a solo transpacific flight. The following year he began his highly publicized effort to become the first person to balloon around the world alone. The initial attempt, however, ended after three days, and a series of subsequent efforts also failed. In 2002 Fossett made his sixth attempt at the record, taking off from Northam, West Australia, in the *Bud Light Spirit of Freedom*. On July 2 he made history as he crossed his starting point, eventually landing in the outback of Queensland.

In 2005 Fossett became the first person to fly an airplane around the world solo without stopping or refueling. Piloting the *GlobalFlyer*, a specialized plane that featured 13 fuel tanks and a 2-metre (7-foot) cockpit, he took off from Salinas, Kansas, on February 28 and returned there some 67 hours later, on March 3. On Feb. 8, 2006, he undertook the longest nonstop airplane flight, taking off from Cape Canaveral, Florida, aboard the *GlobalFlyer*. Some 76 hours later, on February 11, he made an emergency landing in Bournemouth, England, having covered a record 42,469.5 km (26,389.3 miles).

Fossett was also renowned as a speed sailor. In 2001 he recorded the quickest transatlantic crossing—4 days 17 hours 28 minutes 6 seconds—and in 2004 he circumnavigated the globe in an unprecedented time of 58 days 9 hours 32 minutes 45 seconds. By the early 21st century, he had set some 100 records in sailing and aviation. His other achievements included the fastest flight (1,194.17 km, or 742.02 miles, per hour) in a nonsupersonic airplane (2001) as well as a number of gliding records.

On Sept. 3, 2007, Fossett was reported missing after his single-engine plane disappeared during a scouting mission in western Nevada.

Subsequent search efforts were hampered by the area's remoteness and rugged terrain. On Feb. 15, 2008, Fossett was declared dead by a court in Chicago. In October the wreckage of his plane and his remains were found in Inyo National Forest, Nevada.

condition and the immediate forecast govern the decision to launch. Once the balloon is airborne and on its way, the weather model must be constantly updated and the balloon navigated precisely to take advantage of varying conditions. While the aeronauts of the 19th century had balloons that could theoretically cross the Atlantic, all attempts failed because they lacked the meteorology to make accurate predictions and the means to communicate predictions to the balloonist.

AIRSHIPS

Airships are self-propelled, lighter-than-air craft that are also called dirigibles, from the French *diriger*, "to steer." Three main types of airships have been built: nonrigids (blimps), semirigids, and rigids. All three types have four principal parts: a cigar-shaped bag, or balloon, that is filled with a lighter-than-air gas; a car or gondola that is slung beneath the balloon and holds the crew and passengers; engines that drive propellers; and horizontal and vertical rudders to steer the craft. Nonrigids are simply balloons with cars attached by cables; if the gas escapes, the balloon collapses. Semirigids likewise depend on the internal gas to maintain the balloon's shape, but they also have a structural metal keel that extends longitudinally along the balloon's base and supports the car. Rigids consist of a light framework of aluminum-alloy girders that is covered with fabric but is not airtight. Inside this framework are a number of gas-filled balloons, each of which can be filled or emptied separately; rigids keep their shape whether they are filled with gas or not.

The usual gases used for lifting airships are hydrogen and helium. Hydrogen is the lightest known gas and thus has great lifting capacity, but it is also highly flammable and has caused many fatal airship disasters. Helium is not as buoyant but is far safer than hydrogen because it does not burn. The gas-containing envelopes of early airships used cotton fabric impregnated with rubber, a combination that was eventually superseded by synthetic fabrics such as neoprene and Dacron.

The first successful airship was constructed by Henri Giffard of France in 1852. Giffard built a 160-kg (350-pound) steam engine capable of developing 3 horsepower, sufficient to turn a large propeller at 110 revolutions per minute. To carry the engine weight he filled a bag 44 metres (144 feet) long with hydrogen and, ascending from the Paris Hippodrome, flew at a speed of 10 km (6 miles) per hour to cover a distance of about 30 km (20 miles).

In 1872 a German engineer, Paul Haenlein, first used an internal-combustion engine for flight in an airship that used lifting gas from the bag as fuel. In 1883 Albert and Gaston Tissandier of France became the first to successfully power an airship using an electric motor. Alberto Santos-Dumont, a Brazilian living in Paris, set a number of records in a series of 14 nonrigid, gasoline-powered airships that he built from 1898 to 1905.

The first rigid airship, with a hull of aluminum sheeting, was built in Germany in 1897, but the most successful operator of rigid airships was Ferdinand, Count (Graf) von Zeppelin, a retired German army officer. His first completed airship, the LZ-1 (for Luftschiff Zeppelin 1), made its initial flight from a floating hangar on Lake Constance, near Friedrichshafen, Ger., on July 2, 1900. This technically sophisticated craft, 128 metres (420 feet) long and 11.6 metres (38 feet) in diameter, had an aluminum frame of 24 longitudinal girders set within 16 transverse rings. Beneath the craft a keellike structure connected two external cars, each of which contained a 16-horsepower engine geared to two propellers. A sliding weight secured

The airships Hindenburg *and* Graf Zeppelin *over the Reichstag, Berlin, Germany, March 28, 1936.* Encyclopædia Britannica, Inc.

to the keel afforded vertical control by raising or lowering the nose, while rudders were provided for horizontal control. The craft attained speeds approaching 32 km (20 miles) per hour.

Zeppelin continued improving his designs through World War I, when many of his airships (called zeppelins), which could attain higher altitudes than the airplanes then available, were used to bomb Paris and London. Airships were also used by the Allies during the war, chiefly for anti-submarine patrol. A number of zeppelins were distributed to the Allied countries as a part of postwar reparations by Germany.

In the 1920s and '30s airship construction continued in Europe and the United States. A British dirigible, the R-34, made a round-trip transatlantic crossing in July 1919. In 1926 an Italian semirigid airship was successfully used by Roald Amundsen, Lincoln Ellsworth, and General Umberto Nobile to explore the North Pole. In 1928 the *Graf Zeppelin* was completed by Zeppelin's successor, Hugo Eckener, in Germany. Before it was decommissioned nine years later it had made 590 flights, including 144 ocean crossings. and had flown more than 1.6 million km (1 million miles). In 1929 the craft covered about 34,600 km (21,500 miles) in a world flight that was completed in an elapsed time of approximately 21 days.

In 1936 Germany inaugurated a regular transatlantic passenger service with the *Graf Zeppelin* and the giant dirigible *Hindenburg*. Despite these achievements, airships were virtually abandoned in the late 1930s because of their cost, their slow speed, and their intrinsic vulnerability to stormy weather. In addition, a succession of disasters—the best known being the explosion of the hydrogen-filled *Hindenburg* in 1937—coupled with advances in heavier-than-air craft in the 1930s and '40s made dirigibles commercially obsolete for most applications.

THE HINDENBURG DISASTER

The largest rigid airship ever constructed, the *Hindenburg* was launched at Friedrichshafen, Ger., in March 1936. A 245-metre- (804-foot-) long conventional zeppelin design, it was powered by four 1,100-horsepower diesel engines, giving it a maximum speed of 135 km (84 miles) per hour and a cruising speed of 126 km (78 miles) per hour. Though it was designed to be filled with helium gas, the airship was filled with highly flammable hydrogen owing to export restrictions on helium imposed by the United States against Nazi Germany.

In 1936 the *Hindenburg* inaugurated commercial air service across the North Atlantic by carrying 1,002 passengers on 10 scheduled round trips between Germany and the United States. On May 6, 1937, while landing at Lakehurst, N.J., on the first of its scheduled 1937 transatlantic crossings, the *Hindenburg* burst into flames and was completely destroyed. Thirty-six of the 97 persons aboard were killed. The fire was officially attributed to a discharge of atmospheric electricity in the vicinity of a hydrogen gas leak from the airship, though at the time it was speculated that the dirigible was the victim of an anti-Nazi act of sabotage. The *Hindenburg* disaster marked the end of the use of rigid airships in commercial air transportation.

The Zeppelin airship works were destroyed by Allied bombing during World War II, and building of the huge rigid airships was never resumed. In 1993, descendant companies of Luftschiffbau-Zeppelin founded Zeppelin Luftschifftechnik GmbH, which built the Zeppelin NT ("New Technology"), a smaller (75-metre, or 250-foot) helium-filled airship that in 2001 began to offer short sightseeing trips over Lake Constance and other locations.

CHAPTER 3

THE INVENTION OF THE AIRPLANE

On the evening of Sept. 18, 1901, Wilbur Wright, a 33-year-old businessman from Dayton, Ohio, addressed a distinguished group of Chicago engineers on the subject of "Some Aeronautical Experiments" that he had conducted with his brother Orville Wright over the previous two years. "The difficulties which obstruct the pathway to success in flying machine construction," he noted, "are of three general classes":

1. Those relating to the construction of the sustaining wings.
2. Those relating to the generation and application of the power required to drive the machine through the air.
3. Those relating to the balancing and steering of the machine after it is actually in flight.

This clear analysis—the clearest possible statement of the problem of heavier-than-air flight—addressed the three central problems that had to be solved in order to bring about the invention of the airplane: the dynamic reaction of lifting surfaces (or wings), the design of absolutely reliable engines to produce sufficient power to propel an airframe, and the controlling of flight in three dimensions. Once the Wright brothers had demonstrated that the basic technical problems had been overcome at the start of the 20th century, military and civil aviation developed quickly.

THE PROBLEM OF LIFT

The dream of human flight must have begun with observation of birds soaring through the sky. For millennia, however, progress was retarded by attempts to design aircraft that emulated the beating of a bird's wings. The generations of experimenters and dreamers who focused their attention on ornithopters—machines in which flapping wings generated both lift and propulsion—contributed nothing substantial to the final solution of the problems blocking the route to mechanical flight.

Thus, the story of the invention of the airplane begins in the 16th, 17th, and 18th centuries, with the

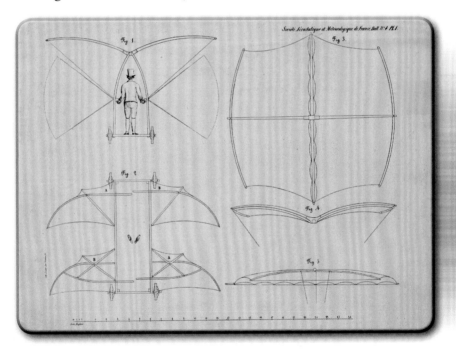

English aeronautic pioneer George Cayley established the modern notion of a fixed-wing aircraft in 1799, and he designed a glider (shown in the drawing) that was safely flown by his reluctant servant in 1853 in the first recorded successful manned flight. Library of Congress, Washington, D.C. (neg. no. LC-DIG-ppmsca-02521)

first serious research into aerodynamics—the study of the forces operating on a solid body (for instance, a wing when it is immersed in a stream of air). Leonardo da Vinci and Galileo Galilei in Italy, Christiaan Huygens in the Netherlands, and Isaac Newton in England all contributed to an understanding of the relationship between resistance (drag) and such factors as the surface area of an object exposed to the stream and the density of a fluid. Swiss mathematicians Daniel Bernoulli and Leonhard Euler and British engineer John Smeaton explained the relationship between pressure and velocity and provided information that enabled a later generation of engineers to calculate aerodynamic forces.

George Cayley, an English baronet, bridged the gap between physical theory, engineering research, and the age-old dream of flight. He gathered critical aerodynamic data of value in the design of winged aircraft, using instruments developed in the 18th century for research into ballistics. Cayley was also a pioneer of aircraft design, explaining that a successful flying machine would have separate systems for lift, propulsion, and control. While he did produce designs for ornithopters, he was the first experimenter to focus on fixed-wing aircraft.

Cayley found the secrets of lift in the shape of a bird's wing, surmising that an arched, or cambered, wing would produce greater lift than a flat wing because of lower pressure on top of the curved surface. His observations of birds in flight led him to recognize the superiority of relatively long and narrow (in modern terminology, high-aspect-ratio) wings for soaring. As a practical matter, however, he designed biplane and multiplane wings (the first of their kind) as a means of providing maximum surface area in a strong and easily braced structure.

Addressing the first meeting of the Aeronautical Society of Great Britain in 1866, Francis H. Wenham provided a concise and forceful restatement of Cayley's most important ideas regarding wings. Five years later, in cooperation with John Browning, Wenham built the first wind tunnel, a device that would have a profound effect on the study of wings and the development of improved airfoils. Horatio Phillips, a fellow member of the Aeronautical Society, developed an even more effective wind tunnel design, and he patented (1884) a two-surface, cambered-airfoil design that provided the foundation for most subsequent work in the field.

Beginning in the 1870s, Otto Lilienthal, a German mechanical engineer, undertook the most important studies of wing design since the time of Cayley. His detailed measurements of the forces operating on a cambered wing at various angles of attack provided precise bits of data employed by later experimenters—including, in the United States, the engineer Octave Chanute and the Wright brothers—to calculate the performance of their own wings. Having published the results of his research, Lilienthal designed, built, and flew a series of monoplane and biplane gliders, completing as many as 2,000 flights between 1890 and the time of his fatal glider crash in August 1896.

At the outset of their own aeronautical experiments, the Wright brothers carefully studied the work of their predecessors and decided that there was little need for them to focus on wing design. "Men already know how to construct wings...," Wilbur explained in 1901, "which when driven through the air at sufficient speed will not only sustain themselves but also that of the engine, and of the engineer as well."

Two years of experimenting with gliders, however, demonstrated the need to pay considerably more attention to wing design. Beginning in November 1901, the Wright brothers used a wind tunnel of their own design to gather information that enabled them to calculate the values of lift and drag for an entire series of airfoils at various angles of attack and to measure the performance of wings with differing aspect ratios, tip shapes, and other design features. That information culminated in the Wright glider of 1902, a breakthrough machine whose wing design enabled the Wright brothers to take the final steps to the invention of the airplane.

THE PROBLEM OF PROPULSION

At the beginning of the 19th century, sustained powered heavier-than-air flight remained an impossibility because of the lack of suitable power plants. The level of technology that would permit even limited powered flight lay over a century in the future. Clockwork mechanisms and other sorts of spring-powered systems were clearly unsuitable for human flight. While electricity powered several airships during the last quarter of the century, the poor power-to-weight ratio of such systems made it difficult to imagine an electrically propelled airplane.

The aeronautical potential of propulsion systems ranging from hot-air engines to gunpowder to compressed air and even to carbonic-acid power plants was discussed during the course of the century. The Australian Lawrence Hargrave, in particular, experimented with compressed-gas propulsion systems. Nevertheless, steam and internal-combustion engines quickly emerged as the choice of most serious experimenters. As early as 1829, F.D. Artingstall constructed a full-scale steam-powered ornithoptor, the wings of which were smashed in operation just before the boiler exploded. A lightweight steam engine developed by the English pioneer Frederick Stringfellow in 1868 to power a triplane model aircraft

THE AERODROME AS SEEN FROM ABOVE.

THE AERODROME AS SEEN FROM BELOW.

THE LANGLEY AERODROME IN FLIGHT.

An artist's rendition of the flight of Samuel Pierpont Langley's steam-powered unmanned aerodrome No. 5 on May 6, 1896, as seen from above and below. © Photos.com/Jupiterimages

survives in the collection of the Smithsonian Institution, Washington, D.C.

Russian Alexandr Mozhaysky (1884), Englishman Hiram Maxim (1894), and Frenchman Clément Ader (1890) each jumped full-scale steam-powered machines off the ground for short distances, although none of these craft was capable of sustained or controlled flight. In the United States, Samuel Pierpont Langley achieved the first sustained flights in 1896 when he launched two of his relatively large steam-powered model aircraft on aerial journeys of up to three-quarters of a mile (1.2 km) over the Potomac River.

As the end of the 19th century approached, the internal-combustion engine emerged as an even more promising aeronautical power plant. The process had begun in 1860, when Étienne Lenoir of Belgium built the first internal-combustion engine, fueled with illuminating gas. In Germany, Nikolaus A. Otto took the next step in 1876, producing a four-stroke engine burning liquid fuel. German engineer Gottlieb Daimler pioneered the development of lightweight high-speed gasoline engines, one of which he mounted on a bicycle in 1885. German engineer Karl Benz produced the first true automobile the following year, a sturdy tricycle with seating for the operator and a passenger. In 1888 Daimler persuaded Karl Woelfert, a Lutheran minister who longed to fly, to equip an experimental airship with a single-cylinder gasoline engine that developed all of eight horsepower. The initial test was marginally successful, although the open-flame ignition system presented an obvious danger to a hydrogen-filled airship. In fact, Woelfert perished when an internal-combustion engine finally did set a much larger airship on fire in 1897.

At the beginning of their career in aeronautics, the Wright brothers recognized that automotive enthusiasts were producing ever lighter and more powerful internal-combustion engines. The brothers assumed that if their gliding experiments progressed to the point where they required a power plant, it would not be difficult to buy or build a gasoline engine for their aircraft.

They were essentially correct. Having flown their successful glider of 1902, the Wright brothers were confident that their wings would lift the weight of a powered flying machine and that they could control such a craft in the air. Moreover, three years of experience with gliders, and the information gathered with their wind tunnel, enabled them to calculate the precise amount of power required for sustained flight. Unable to interest an experienced manufacturer in producing an engine meeting their relatively narrow power-for-weight specifications, the brothers designed and built their own power plant.

Charles Taylor, a machinist whom the brothers employed in their bicycle shop, produced a four-cylinder engine with a cast aluminum block that produced roughly 12.5 horsepower at a total weight of some 90 kg (200 pounds), including fuel and coolant. It was by no means the most advanced or efficient aeronautical power plant

Orville Wright beginning the first successful controlled flight in history, at Kill Devil Hills, North Carolina, Dec. 17, 1903. Courtesy of National Air and Space Museum, Smithsonian Institution, Washington, D.C.

THE WRIGHT BROTHERS AT KITTY HAWK

The first powered airplane to demonstrate sustained flight under the full control of the pilot was the Wright brothers' flyer of 1903. Designed and built by Wilbur and Orville in Dayton, Ohio, it was assembled in the autumn of 1903 at a camp at the base of the Kill Devil Hills, near Kitty Hawk, a village on the Outer Banks of North Carolina. After a first attempt failed on December 14, the machine was flown four times on December 17, to distances of 120, 175, 200, and 852 feet (36.6, 53.3, 61, and 260 metres), respectively. It is now on display in the National Air and Space Museum of the Smithsonian Institution, Washington, D.C.

The 1903 Wright airplane was an extremely strong yet flexible braced biplane structure. Forward of the wings was a twin-surface horizontal elevator, and to the rear was a twin-surface vertical rudder. Wing spars and other long, straight sections of the craft were constructed of spruce, while the wing ribs and other bent or shaped pieces were built of ash. Aerodynamic surfaces were covered with a finely woven muslin cloth. The flyer was propelled by a four-cylinder gasoline engine of the Wrights' own design that developed some 12.5 horsepower after the first few seconds of operation. The engine was linked through a chain-drive transmission to twin contrarotating pusher propellers, which it turned at an average speed of 348 rotations per minute.

The pilot lay on the lower wing of the biplane with his hips positioned in a padded wooden cradle. A movement of the hips to the right or left operated the "wing-warping" system, which increased the angle of attack of the wings on one side of the craft and decreased it on the other, enabling the pilot to raise or lower the wing tips on either side in order to maintain balance or to roll into a turn. A small hand lever controlled the forward elevator, which provided pitch control and some extra lift. The rear rudder was directly linked to the wing-warping system in order to counteract problems of yaw produced by the warping of the wings.

The Wrights knew that it would be difficult to operate a wheeled aircraft from the rough and sandy surface where they planned to fly, so they decided to launch their machine into the air with a smooth run down a 60-foot (18-metre)-long monorail track. The launch rail consisted of four 15-foot (4.5-metre) two-by-fours, the thin upper edge of which was protected by a metal cap strip. The airplane ran down the rail on two modified bicycle wheel hubs.

At the beginning of each flight the airplane was positioned at the head of the rail. A restraining line ran from a clip near the pilot's position at the leading edge of the lower wing to a stake driven into the ground behind the machine. The engine could not be throttled; a hand lever only allowed the pilot to open or close the fuel line. In order to start the engine, a coil box was connected to the spark plugs, and two men pulled the propellers through to turn the engine over. When the pilot was ready, he released the restraining rope with the hand clip, and the machine moved down the rail.

The 1903 machine was never flown after December 17. While sitting on the ground after the fourth flight, it was flipped by a gust of wind and badly damaged. Shipped back to Dayton, it was reassembled and repaired as needed for temporary exhibitions before being put on display at the Science Museum, London, in 1928. There it remained for 20 years, at the centre of a dispute between Orville Wright and the Smithsonian Institution over claims that the Institution's third secretary, Samuel P. Langley, had constructed a machine capable of flight prior to the Wrights' flights of December 1903. The dispute ended with an apology from the Smithsonian in 1942, and the flyer was transferred permanently to the Institution's collection in 1948, several months after Orville's death.

in the world. Langley, who was also building a full-scale powered flying machine, spent thousands of dollars to produce a five-cylinder radial engine with a total weight equal to that of the Wright engine but developing 52.4 horsepower. Langley produced an engine far superior to that of the Wright brothers—and an airplane, the aerodrome No. 6, that failed to fly when tested in 1903. The Wright brothers, on the other hand, developed an engine that produced exactly the power required to propel their flyer of 1903—the world's first airplane to demonstrate sustained flight.

The design of the propellers for the 1903 airplane represented a much more difficult task, and a much greater technical achievement, than the development of the engine. The propellers not only had to be efficient but had to produce a calculated amount of thrust when operated at a particular speed by the engine. It is important to recognize, however, that once powered flight had been achieved, the development of more powerful and efficient engines became an essential element in the drive to improve aircraft performance.

THE PROBLEM OF CONTROL

Having decided that the design of wings and the development of a power plant were fairly well in hand, the Wright brothers focused on the element of control. Other experimenters had given some thought to the subject. Cayley was the first to use an elevator for control in pitch (directing the nose up and down). Throughout the second half of the 19th century, airships had used rudders for yaw control (directing the nose to the right and left).

It was far more difficult to conceive of a way to control an aircraft in roll (that is, balancing the wingtips or banking the aircraft). Moreover, most experimenters were convinced that the operator of a flying machine would find it difficult or impossible to exercise full control over a machine that was free to operate in all three axes of motion at once. As a result, far more thought had been given to the means of achieving automatic or inherent stability than to active control systems.

Cayley, for example, suggested dihedral wings (wingtips angled up from the midpoint of the wing) as a means of achieving a measure of stability in roll; he also recommended the use of a pendulum to control pitch. French aviation pioneer Alphonse Penaud was the first to produce an inherently stable aircraft, the Planophore (1871), which featured a pusher propeller powered by twisted rubber strands. The hand-launched model featured dihedral wings for stability in roll and a horizontal surface set at a slight negative angle with regard to the wings to provide stability in pitch. With the addition of a vertical surface for stability in yaw, this was the approach taken by virtually all experimenters with model aircraft, including Langley.

Model builders were forced to employ automatic stability, but those experimenters who built and flew gliders had to develop active flight controls. Virtually all of the pre-Wright brothers glider pilots, including Lilienthal, used hang-gliding techniques, in which the pilot shifted his weight in order to alter the position of the centre of gravity of the machine with regard to the centre of pressure. Weight shifting was dangerous and limiting, however. If simple movements of the operator's body were to have a significant impact on the motion of the machine, the wing area had to be reasonably small. This limited the amount of lift that could be generated. Moreover, it was by no means difficult for such an aircraft to reach a stall or some other uncontrolled position from which weight shifting could not effect a recovery—as demonstrated by the deaths of Lilienthal (1896) and the English experimenter Percy Pilcher (1899) in glider crashes.

Determined to avoid those problems, the Wright brothers created a positive control system that enabled (indeed, required) the pilot to exercise absolute command over the motion of his machine in every axis and at every moment. Others had rejected that goal because they feared that pilots would be overwhelmed by the difficulty of controlling a machine moving in three dimensions. The

Wright brothers, however, had recognized how easily and quickly a bicycle rider internalized the motions required to maintain balance and control, and they were certain that it would be the same with an airplane.

Recognizing the dangers inherent in attempting to rely on control of the centre of gravity, the Wright brothers devised a system to control the movement of the centre of pressure on the wing. They achieved this by enabling the pilot to induce a twist across the upper and lower wings in either direction, thus increasing the lift on one side and decreasing it on the other. This technique, which they called "wing warping," solved the crucial problem of roll. Meanwhile, an elevator (a horizontal surface placed at the front of the aircraft) provided the means of pitch control. When the Wright brothers introduced a rudder to their design in 1902, this device was used to compensate for increased drag on the positively warped side of the aircraft. In 1905 they disconnected the rudder from the wing warping system, enabling the pilot to exercise independent control in yaw for the first time. The Wright flyer of 1905 is therefore considered to be the first fully controllable, practical airplane.

OTHER AVIATION PIONEERS

The work of the Wright brothers inspired an entire generation of flying-machine experimenters in Europe and the Americas. The Brazilian experimenter Alberto Santos-Dumont, for instance, made the first public flight in Europe in 1906 in his 14-*bis*. Frenchman Henri Farman made his first flight the following year in the Farman III, a machine built by Gabriel Voisin. Farman also completed

On Jan. 13, 1908, French aviator Henri Farman won the Grand Prix d'Aviation for the first circular flight of more than 1 km (0.6 mile). Library of Congress, Washington, D.C. (neg. no. LC-DIG-ggbain-04183)

the first European circular flight of at least 1 km (0.62 mile) early in 1908. On July 4, 1908, the American Glenn Hammond Curtiss, a leading member of the Aerial Experiment Association (AEA), organized by Alexander Graham Bell, won the Scientific American Trophy for a flight of 1 km in the AEA June Bug.

The Santos-Dumont, Voisin, and Curtiss machines were all canard (elevator on the nose) biplanes with pusher propellers that were clearly inspired by what the designers knew of the work of the Wright brothers.

By 1909 radical new monoplane designs had taken to the air, built and flown by men such as the French pioneers Robert Esnault-Pelterie and Louis Blériot, both of whom

American aeronautic pioneer Glenn Hammond Curtiss piloted his Model E flying boat over Keuka Lake, near Hammondsport, N.Y., in 1912. Library of Congress, Washington, D.C. (neg. no. LC-DIG-ggbain-11555)

were involved in the development of the "stick-and-rudder" cockpit control system that would soon be adopted by other builders. Blériot brought the early experimental era of aviation to an end on July 25, 1909, when he flew his Type XI monoplane across the English Channel.

The following five years, from Blériot's Channel flight to the beginning of World War I, were a period of spectacular growth and development in aviation. Concerned about the potential of military aviation, European leaders invested heavily in the new technology, spending large sums on research and development and working to establish and support the aircraft and engine industries in their own countries. In addition to practical developments in the areas of propulsion and aircraft structural design, the foundations of modern aerodynamic theory were laid by scientists and academics such as Ludwig Prandtl of

French aviation pioneer Robert Esnault-Pelterie designed, built, and was the first to fly the R.E.P. No. 2, in 1908. Library of Congress, Washington, D.C. (neg. no. LC-DIG-ggbain-04136)

Germany. With the possible exception of flying boats, an area in which Curtiss continued to dominate, leadership in virtually every phase of aeronautics had passed by 1910 from the United States to Europe, where it would remain throughout World War I.

CHAPTER 4

PISTONS AND PROPELLERS

During World War I several farsighted European entrepreneurs, emboldened by wartime progress in aviation, envisioned the possibilities of postwar airline travel. For many months after the war, normal rail travel in Europe remained problematic and irregular because of the shortage of passenger equipment and the destruction of tracks and bridges. In addition, chaotic political conditions in central and eastern Europe often disrupted schedules. The situation opened many possibilities for launching airline routes.

Although few airfields existed, aircraft of the postwar era could and did use relatively short sod runways for years, meaning that locating suitable airports near most cities was not the formidable engineering challenge that emerged in subsequent decades. Characteristically, organizers of the first postwar airlines relied on stocks of inexpensive surplus military planes, especially bombers, such as the De Havilland DH-4, that could be modified to accommodate passengers and mail. Two basic types of piston engines powered the typical fabric-covered biplanes of the early postwar era. In-line engines, with cylinders aligned one behind the other or positioned in two banks in a V-type installation, required a radiator and the circulation of a liquid coolant. Radial engines, with cylinders arranged in a circle around the crankshaft, had numerous small fins on the cylinder that radiated heat to the passing airstream in order to keep the engine cool. These relatively straightforward piston-engine designs made long-range flights possible and opened a new era of passenger travel.

THE HEADLINERS

Although airlines ran newspaper advertisements after World War I, the biggest aviation headlines belonged to fliers in relatively primitive piston-engine aircraft that challenged the Atlantic and transcontinental distances. In May 1919 a U.S. Navy Curtiss NC-4 (successor to the Curtiss Model E flying boat) made it from Newfoundland to Portugal by way of the Azores Islands before flying on to Great Britain, compiling 54 hours 31 minutes in the air over its 23-day trip. The following month, former British Royal Air Force (RAF) pilots John Alcock and Arthur Brown made the first nonstop crossing of the Atlantic, requiring 16 hours 28 minutes for the journey from Newfoundland to Ireland in a Vickers Vimy bomber.

By 1924 the U.S. Army had completed plans to make the first aerial circumnavigation of the world, sending a quartet of single-engine Douglas "World Cruisers" westward toward Asia. These fabric-covered biplanes featured interchangeable landing gear—replacing wheels with floats for water landings. One plane crashed in Alaska, forcing the two-man crew to hike out of a snowbound wilderness. Near the end of the expedition, a second aircraft, en route to Iceland, went down between the Orkney and Faroe islands. With support from the U.S. Navy, U.S. State Department, and overseas American officials during an odyssey of 37,622 km (23,377 miles) that consumed 175 days, the remaining pair of planes arrived back in Seattle. All this happened before Charles Lindbergh, flying a single-engine Ryan monoplane, made his nonstop solo flight in 33 hours 30 minutes from New York to Paris in

The Vickers Vimy plane used by John Alcock and Arthur Brown in the first nonstop transatlantic flight.

1927. Lindbergh's flight, in particular, demonstrated the essential reliability of improved radial engines.

In Britain, overland flights connecting colonial interests down the length of Africa drew considerable attention. Departing London, another pair of ex-RAF pilots battled capricious winds, sudden storms, equatorial updrafts, and assorted adventures before arriving at Cape Town after 45 days and three planes. Alan Cobham repeated the feat in a single-engine commercial plane, surveying a route for Imperial Airways, Ltd., from 1925 to 1926. Other British pilots persevered in reaching Australia by way of India (brothers Ross and Keith Smith, 1919) and across the Pacific (Charles Kingsford Smith and Charles Ulm, 1928). The challenge of polar flights also engaged a number of daring fliers. Piloting a Fokker trimotor, Richard Byrd made claim to the first flight over the North Pole in 1926, followed by his pioneering expedition with a Ford Motor Company trimotor over the South Pole in 1929.

The 1930s brought a new round of record flights by Americans. In 1931, with navigator Harold Gatty, Wiley

LINDBERGH CROSSES THE ATLANTIC

Charles A. Lindbergh's early years were spent chiefly in Little Falls, Minn., and in Washington, D.C., where for 10 years his father represented the 6th district of Minnesota in Congress. His formal education ended during his second year at the University of Wisconsin in Madison, when his growing interest in aviation led to enrollment in a flying school in Lincoln, Neb., and the purchase of a World War I Curtiss Jenny, with which he made stunt-flying tours through Southern and Midwestern states. After a year at the army flying schools in Texas (1924–25), he became an airmail pilot (1926), flying the route from St. Louis, Mo., to Chicago. During this period he obtained financial backing from a group of St. Louis businessmen to compete for the $25,000 prize offered for the first nonstop flight between New York and Paris. In the monoplane *Spirit of St. Louis* he made the 3,610-mile (5,810-km) flight in 33.5 hours on May 20–21, 1927. Overnight Lindbergh became a folk hero on both sides of the Atlantic, and public enthusiasm for flying and aircraft exploded (a phenomenon dubbed the "Lindbergh boom").

Lindbergh's plane was a Ryan NYP ("New York to Paris"), modified from the Ryan M2, a single-engine, high-wing monoplane designed for mail and passenger service by T. Claude Ryan of Ryan Airlines, San Diego, Calif. In standard conformation the airplane would have seated five people; extra fuel tanks in the *Spirit of St. Louis* occupied much of what had been cabin space. The windshield was replaced by an extension of the nose cowling, so that Lindbergh had direct vision only from the side windows, relying on a periscope to see straight ahead. There was no radio. A Wright Whirlwind air-cooled radial engine developed a maximum of 237 horsepower. Wing-span of the craft was 46 feet (14 metres) and length 27 feet 8 inches (8.4 metres). Fuel capacity with the extra tanks was 450 gallons; top speed at sea level, when loaded, was 120 miles (200 km) per hour, and range was 4,100 miles (6,600 km).

The *Spirit of St. Louis* was returned from Europe to the United States aboard ship, and Lindbergh flew it extensively throughout North, Central, and South America to promote interest in aeronautics before donating it to the Smithsonian Institution. It resides today in the National Air and Space Museum, keeping company with the Wright brothers' 1903 flyer.

Post piloted a Lockheed Vega 5B monoplane (named *Winnie Mae* for Post's daughter) around the world in slightly less than 8 days 16 hours. Two years later, with the aid of an autopilot, Post broke his world record during a solo flight of 7 days 19 hours. In 1932 Amelia Earhart became the first woman to complete a solo transatlantic flight. Five years later, during a global attempt, she disappeared somewhere over the Pacific. Aviator and industrialist Howard Hughes, piloting a twin-engine Lockheed Model 14 (similar to Earhart's Lockheed 5B Vega airplane) with a four-man crew, completed a global flight in 1938 in the record time of slightly more than 3 days 19 hours. Flights like these demonstrated aviation's ability to overcome geographic barriers and shrink time-distance relationships.

In addition to long-distance records, speed records continued to rise. For example, the Schneider Trophy races, conducted in Europe between 1913 and 1931, pitted single-engine racing planes equipped with floats against each other. With entrants carrying the colours of their respective countries, considerable international prestige and technological recognition was attached to the outcome. Designers focused on high-performance engines and streamlined fuselages. By the early 1930s, successful British racers from Supermarine, reaching about 340 miles (550 km) per hour, were contributing to the designs that led to the legendary Spitfire fighters of World War II. Behind the headlines, the collective technology and operational know-how of the record-seekers contributed to modern airline travel.

THE FIRST AIRLINES

One of the earliest airline organizations, a British group called Air Transport and Travel, Ltd., acquired several Airco D.H.4a VIII single-engine planes (designed by

Geoffrey De Havilland), powered by 350-horsepower Eagle V-type engines from Rolls-Royce, Ltd., and modified them to include an enclosed cramped space in the fuselage with room for two adventurous passengers. The pilot's cockpit, atop the fuselage, remained open. The company's inaugural flight occurred on Aug. 25, 1919, when the plane flew from London to Paris with its sole passenger, an enterprising newspaper reporter.

The service caught on and competitors soon followed. Handley Page Transport, Ltd., made use of the manufacturing company's wartime twin-engine bombers, converting them to haul up to 14 passengers, who lounged in comfortable wicker chairs. These slow but roomy aircraft established a tradition of ornately embellished interiors and spacious surroundings—at the sacrifice of aerodynamic efficiency and high speeds—on early European airlines. Given the lack of navigational aids and the primitive instrumentation of the era, accidents invariably occurred, and passengers became used to delays caused by the notoriously foul winter weather in England. Pilots had to depend on luck and quick thinking when they were caught in unexpected atmospheric conditions. Approaching London in the fog, one British pilot suddenly realized he had drifted too close to the ground when a church steeple loomed out of the mist at his eye level. Fortunately, he noticed that express trains speeding toward London left a visible furrow in the dense fog bank, and he gratefully followed this phenomenon into the city, where he found improved conditions for landing. By 1924, with government support, independent airlines in Britain had consolidated into one entity, Imperial Airways, Ltd., as a means to compete with the heavily subsidized French airlines in Europe.

The British also used airlines to knit together elements of their far-flung empire. During the 1920s,

Imperial Airways, Ltd., employees refueling a Handley Page H.P.42 airliner at Semakh on the Sea of Galilee, 1931. Library of Congress, Washington, D.C. (neg. no. LC-M32- 4239)

Imperial Airways mounted operations in Africa and the Middle East. Across trackless stretches of sparsely inhabited desert, creative surveyor crews shrewdly drove cars and trucks to create a visible track for pilots to follow; in some areas, they plowed furrows in the ground. Into the late 1930s, standard equipment on these routes was the stately Handley Page H.P.42, a biplane having a wingspan of 40 metres (130 feet) and four 490-horsepower Bristol Jupiter engines. Depending on seating arrangements, 24 to 38 passengers cruised along at about 160 km (100 miles) per hour over the plane's 800-km (500-mile) range. The airline scheduled several days (including overnight stops) to travel from London to the Cape of South Africa by air, compared with some weeks by steamship. The route's clientele characteristically included well-placed colonial officials and wealthy business travelers who expected first-class service. Consequently, the H.P.42's passenger cabin featured dimensions nearly equal to the size of a Pullman railway car, and patrons appreciated plush wall-to-wall carpeting and a stand-up bar. Attentive stewards served seven-course meals.

France also had territorial possessions in Africa as well as important business interests in Latin America. Consequently, French airlines ran along the Mediterranean coast of Spain, over to Morocco, and down the western coast of Africa as far as Dakar, Seneg. The routes took planes and crews over some of the most inhospitable areas of northwest Africa, where native tribesmen maintained strong prejudices against Europeans. Forced down in the desert, some French airmen were killed, and others were carted off in cages to be held as hostages for ransom. Antoine de Saint-Exupéry, the famed aviator and author, became successful as a field manager in Africa, donning native garb and negotiating peace with local tribal chiefs. A bewildering variety of planes from Henri Farman, Louis-Charles Bréguet, Pierre Latécoère, and others equipped domestic and international airlines. By the 1930s, the French had also established operations in South America and begun to experiment with mail deliveries across the South Atlantic.

In 1919 the Netherlands organized a new airline, KLM, and began service between London and Amsterdam using aircraft built by Anthony Fokker. (KLM now proudly claims the title of the world's oldest continuously operating airline.) By 1930, KLM offered weekly service to Batavia (now Jakarta), the colonial capital of the Dutch East Indies, and competed with Imperial Airways in the Far East. Pioneering air services also sprang up in Africa, Asia, and Australia.

Germany, prevented by the Treaty of Versailles from developing military aircraft, poured considerable effort into civilian designs. The German government also gave its blessing to the expansionist plans of Deutsche Luft Hansa (now Deutsche Lufthansa Ag), formed in 1926. Hugo Junkers's firm supplied a steady stream of low-wing single- and three-engine planes, clad in corrugated metal, that survived for decades in obscure corners of the world. Meanwhile, German airliners became regular callers throughout central and eastern Europe, with routes that extended as far east as Moscow. Other segments of Lufthansa covered Scandinavia and the Baltic; still others ran to the eastern Mediterranean and down to Baghdad. By the mid-1930s, Germany operated the largest commercial airline network in Europe.

Out of the chaos of World War I, imperial Russia emerged as the Union of Soviet Socialist Republics. The communist regime soon seized on aviation as an icon of a new technical world to be shaped by the industrial proletariat. Aeroflot, the state airline, not only served propaganda purposes but subsequently emerged as an indispensable medium for rapid transportation and a visible means of knitting together the sprawling, divergent regions of the Soviet Union. Although the Soviet regime occasionally purchased western technology, its commissars emphasized the use of indigenous equipment in order to be free of invidious capitalistic influences. Consequently, Soviet engine and aircraft design bureaus, like that run by Oleg Antonov, turned out hundreds of planes for use on Aeroflot's vast internal airway system.

FROM AIRMAIL TO AIRLINES IN THE UNITED STATES

Although the American experience sometimes reflected European trends, it also demonstrated clear differences. Under the auspices of the U.S. Postal Service, an airmail operation was launched in 1918 as a wartime effort to stimulate aircraft production and to generate a pool of trained pilots. Using Curtiss JN-4H ("Jenny") trainers converted to mail planes, the early service floundered. After the war, shrewd airmail bureaucrats obtained larger American-built De Havilland DH-4 biplanes with liquid-cooled Liberty engines from surplus military stocks. Their top speed of 80 miles (130 km) per hour surpassed the 75 miles (120 km) per hour of the Jenny, allowing mail planes to beat railway delivery times over long distances. By 1924, coast-to-coast airmail service had developed, using light beacons to guide open-cockpit planes at night. Correspondence from New York now arrived on the West Coast in two days instead of five days by railway. This savings in time had a distinct impact on expediting the clearance of checks, interest-bearing securities, and other business paper with a time-sensitive value in transfer between businesses and financial institutions.

Having established a workable airmail system and a considerable clientele, the Postal Service yielded to congressional pressures and, with the Contract Air Mail Act of 1925, turned over the mail service to private contractors. The following year, the Air Commerce Act established a bureau to enforce procedures for the licensing of aircraft, engines, pilots, and other personnel. The former act stimulated design and production of advanced planes to compete with rival carriers; the latter reassured insurance companies, private investors, and banks that safety standards would be enforced. With these elements in hand, American aviation rapidly progressed. Ironically, at the same time that European countries organized subsidized national flag lines and followed practices that often discouraged innovation in the design of airliners, the United States turned over civil aviation to commercial operators, where aggressive competition accelerated significant developments in aviation technology and air-craft performance.

For one thing, manufacturers of airplane motors began a significant period of development in modern piston engines. Because liquid-cooled in-line engines offered less frontal surface, they were often favoured by military designers. With these engines, aircraft could be stream-lined to improve speed but with a trade-off in complexity and weight because of the requisite coolant, coolant lines, radiator, and associated pumps. Air-cooled radial designs, in contrast, achieved relative simplicity, reliability, and comparatively light weight at the cost of more air resis-tance (creating drag) because of their blunt shape. In 1928, the National Advisory Committee for Aeronautics (NACA) announced its famous cowling for radial engines. It not only smoothed airflow around the engine, substan-tially reducing drag, but also enhanced the cooling of the cylinders. With their dependability and ease of main-tenance, radial engines became the type most favoured by designers of American air transports. The Curtiss-Wright Corporation (formed from the merger of Curtiss Aeroplane and Motor Company and Wright Aeronautical in 1929) produced a series of Whirlwind and Cyclone radial engines; Pratt & Whitney Aircraft launched its Wasp designs. Many of these American radial engines powered airplanes built overseas. By the end of the 1930s, innova-tions such as variable-pitch propellers, superchargers (to enhance high-altitude engine performance), and high-octane fuels had contributed to dramatically improved performance in both liquid-cooled and air-cooled radial engines.

During the late 1920s and early 1930s, the U.S. Postal Service instituted payment formulas that favoured aircraft large enough to carry passengers as well as mail. A rising volume of research reports from the NACA facilitated many improved aircraft designs. The result was a swift increase in larger planes with improved radial engines and a shift from biplanes to trimotor monoplane transports marketed by a subsidiary of Ford and by the European builder, Anthony Fokker, who had set up shop in the United States.

Largely owing to airline rivalry, American technology had already taken a major step forward with the introduction of the Boeing Company Model 247 airliner, which cruised at about 180 miles (290 km) per hour and entered service with United Airlines, Inc., in 1933. With its all-metal stressed-skin construction (which used the metal skin covering itself to carry aerodynamic loads), retractable gear, two 550-horsepower Pratt & Whitney Wasp radial engines, and cowlings inspired by NACA research, the 10-passenger Model 247 seemed to be head-and-shoulders above competitive aircraft.

Shortly before the 247 began flying, a Fokker trimotor of Transcontinental & Western Air, Inc. (TWA), crashed in a Kansas farm field. Everybody aboard died, including the University of Notre Dame's revered football coach Knute Rockne. Subsequent investigation of the crash raised questions about structural weakness in the plane's main wooden-wing spar. Controversy about "wooden airplanes" and criticism of the Fokker plane generally gave trimotor airliners a bad image. When TWA asked manufacturers to submit designs for a replacement, Douglas Aircraft Company (later McDonnell Douglas Corporation) responded with an all-metal twin-engine airliner. The DC-2, with an advanced NACA cowling, refined streamlining, and other improvements, mounted Wright Cyclone engines and carried 14 passengers, surpassing the Boeing 247 in every way. Significantly, leading European airlines such as KLM acquired the new Douglas transport, beginning a trend for European operators to buy American

THE DC-3

The Douglas Aircraft Company's DC-3 was a low-wing, twin-engine monoplane with retractable landing gear that in various conformations could seat 21 or 28 passengers or carry 6,000 pounds (2,725 kg) of cargo. Its cruising range was 1,500–2,100 miles (2,400–3,350 km). From its first appearance in 1935, it dominated the infant airline business. In the mid-1940s all but 25 of the 300 airline planes operating in the United States were DC-3s. In civilian service, the plane was operated by a two-man crew, usually with a cabin attendant.

Pilots, both military and civilian, loved the DC-3. It took off easily, cruised comfortably at 185 miles (300 km) per hour at 10,000 feet (3,000 metres), and had a low stalling speed of 67 miles (107 km) per hour. Pilots said it landed itself, and it could fly on only one engine. With stressed aluminum sheathing, it was a strong plane. When production of the DC-3 ended in 1945, more than 13,000 of them had been built. It is frequently said that flying was a curiosity when the DC-3 was first built but was standard transportation when it ceased production. The DC-3's ease of handling and maintenance, its facility at taking off and landing on short runways, and its remarkable reliability combined to keep it flying in many parts of the world into the 21st century.

The DC-3's World War II version, designated the C-47, was simple and effective. It was used to transport passengers (28), fully armed paratroopers (28), wounded troops (18 stretchers and a medical crew of three), military cargo (e.g., two light trucks), and anything else that could fit through its cargo doors and weighed not much more than three tons. The airplane was also used to tow gliders and was even converted to an efficient, high-speed glider by simply removing its engines (and fairing over their empty cowls) and other nonessential weight.

equipment. A subsequent model, the legendary DC-3, entering service in 1936, mounted 1,000-horsepower Cyclone or Wright Wasp radial engines, cruised at 185 miles (300 km) per hour, and carried 21 passengers—double the capacity of the Boeing 247. By 1939, with superior seat capacity, performance, and ancillary refinements,

DC-3 transports already were carrying 90 percent of the world's airline traffic.

While the Douglas transports dramatically improved air travel within the United States and along European routes, airline entrepreneurs kept looking for a vehicle for transoceanic travel. Many in the 1930s still believed that huge gas-filled airships would be the key. Germany built diesel-powered hydrogen-filled airships, or dirigibles, such as the *Hindenburg*, which flew North Atlantic schedules between Europe and the United States during the summer months. American Airlines, Inc., publicized special schedules that allowed DC-3 passengers to make transatlantic connections with the *Hindenburg*'s terminus in New Jersey. This short-lived arrangement ended with the *Hindenburg*'s tragic and fiery destruction upon its arrival from Europe to open the 1937 travel season. Plans for utilizing dirigibles as passenger liners quickly faded.

That left flying boats. Pan American World Airways, Inc. (Pan Am), purchased a number of designs from the Russian-born American engineer Igor Sikorsky. Pan Am operated them on overwater routes in the Caribbean region, often saving weeks of travel time when compared with steamship and railway connections. By the late 1930s, American manufacturers such as the Martin Company (now the Martin Marietta Corporation), Sikorsky, and Boeing were all producing very large four-engine flying boats intended for service over the Atlantic and Pacific. In 1935, using islands strung across the Pacific, Pan Am completed installation of stopover passenger facilities and its own radio communications and meteorological network. With Martin flying boats, most flights carried mail, along with occasional government or business passengers who could pay the high fares.

Inaugural departures occasioned considerable fanfare. In 1939 Eleanor Roosevelt, wife of U.S. President Franklin

Eleanor Roosevelt christens the Pan American flying boat Yankee Clipper at Anacosta Naval Station in 1939. Thomas D. McAvoy/Time & Life Pictures/Getty Images

D. Roosevelt, smashed a bottle of champagne over the bow of an imposing Yankee Clipper flying boat to launch scheduled airmail and luxury passenger service across the Atlantic to Europe. These promising, if expensive, travel innovations were soon curtailed by wartime conditions in Asia and Europe. In any case, progress in long-range land-based four-engine airliners represented advanced engineering that would have soon displaced flying boats.

Fortuitously, the widespread boundaries of the United States contained a growing number of urban complexes with intervening distances that made airline service a desirable option. American transport designs tended to favour more speed for time-conscious passengers. In comparison, airways within the closer boundaries of western Europe favoured short-haul service, often trading speed for luxury, even on longer colonial routes where state subsidies deflected technological competition.

Boeing's Stratoliner, a pathbreaking transport that featured a pressurized cabin, entered service in 1940. Pressurization enabled airliners to fly above adverse weather, permitting transports to maintain dependable schedules and giving passengers a more comfortable trip. Moreover, at higher altitudes, airliners actually experienced less atmospheric friction, or drag, enhancing their performance and fuel efficiency. Only a few Stratoliners entered service before World War II led Boeing to focus on building bombers.

Meanwhile, Douglas had introduced the DC-4. Although it was unpressurized, it possessed a comparable performance to the Stratoliner and could carry more passengers. Also, the DC-4 had a tricycle landing gear (unlike the Stratoliner's conventional tail wheel), which facilitated boarding of passengers, improved the pilots' view of the runway and surrounding airport environment, and enhanced the plane's takeoff characteristics. The DC-4 achieved production status (as the C-54) during the war as the U.S. Army Air Forces' principal long-range transport. Late in the conflict, it was joined by the Lockheed L-049 Constellation (instantly identifiable by its triple vertical fins), originally designed in 1939 as a commercial airliner that blended a pressurized fuselage, tricycle landing gear, and other state-of-the-art features. Characteristics of these sophisticated civilian planes gave the United States a major advantage in postwar airliner competition.

THE AERONAUTICAL INFRASTRUCTURE

The impressive development of airlines and scheduled air travel rested heavily on the evolution of an aeronautical infrastructure. With roots in the late 19th century, European laboratories set the pace in theoretical aeronautical research, but the NACA, established in 1915, soon evolved as one of the world's leading aeronautical centres. The creation of specialized organizations to investigate accidents, determine the probable cause, and make recommendations to avoid repetition played a key role in the improvement of safe air travel.

In the United States, the Daniel Guggenheim Fund for the Promotion of Aeronautics, a private organization, spearheaded a milestone experiment in 1928 in which the pilot's responses to a combination of electronic signals and airplane instruments permitted the first successful "blind flight." This technique represented a huge step forward for aviation. It meant that airlines could sustain schedules that required flying at night. It also meant that planes could fly in many weather conditions that had previously forced pilots to stay grounded or make unscheduled landings. Moreover, the Guggenheim Fund accelerated the science of meteorology for weather forecasting, codification of aeronautical law, and the establishment of college-level aeronautical engineering departments (as well as university research laboratories) that educated essential cadres of aeronautical engineers and scientists.

By the end of the 1920s, most major cities in the United States had established municipal airports. During the depression decade that followed, various New Deal government construction programs improved and built additional airfields with paved all-weather runways. Under federal guidance, major airfields also acquired control towers and radio equipment as part of an air traffic control system meant to ensure safe aircraft movements within an increasingly busy air space. With a bureaucratic framework and essential flight technologies, a basic aeronautical infrastructure had emerged. The stage was set for the introduction of truly modern airliners and their indelible impact on passenger travel.

WARTIME LEGACIES

In 1937 Japan began full-scale offensives against China. European hostilities commenced in 1939, and the United States became involved in World War II in 1941. In Europe, neutral countries such as Sweden, Switzerland, Portugal, and Spain hosted international routes on a limited basis, but the vagaries of war virtually ended regularly scheduled flights until the end of the conflict in 1945. The United States supplied the majority of air transports for Allied forces. The reasons for this were quite straightforward: The DC-3 had already demonstrated its virtuosity, the superior DC-4 was entering service, and the country's prodigious production capability could satisfy most requirements. Drafted into military service, the C-47 (DC-3) and the four-engine C-54 (DC-4) became the workhorses for the U.S., Britain and its Commonwealth, and air-transport units of European governments-in-exile.

As a harbinger of things to come, the wartime achievements of the U.S. Army Air Force Air Transport Command (ATC) constituted a major step forward. The ATC became legendary during its transport services across the towering Himalayan mountain ranges (pilots called these challenging missions "flying the hump"), carrying crucial supplies to Chinese and Allied forces in the China-Burma-India theatre. More important, the ATC operated a global network, establishing airfields, communication centres, and weather-forecasting facilities that pioneered a sustained system of air transportation on an intercontinental basis. The time required to reach destinations around the world contracted dramatically, from a journey of weeks to only a few days, or, within most combat theatres, to a few hours. Transoceanic travel became a matter of routine; at its peak of operations, ATC planes crossed the Atlantic at an average rate of one every 13 minutes.

Anticipating the impact of postwar airlines, many knowledgeable authorities advocated worldwide protocols to normalize flying procedures and legal issues so as to promote an orderly implementation of foreign and intercontinental air routes. In 1944, during a historic meeting convened in Chicago, international representatives eventually agreed on a provisional administrative entity. By 1947, the full-fledged International Civil Aviation Organization (ICAO) had settled in Montreal as an adjunct of the new United Nations organization. The ICAO specified English as the universal language for pilots and air traffic controllers engaged in international operations. Additional protocols specified standardized formats for terminology, radio frequencies, navigational equipment, emergency procedures, runway markings, and airport lighting. Without these protocols, global air travel would have experienced a chaotic—and unacceptably dangerous—evolution.

POSTWAR AIRLINES

After the war, many airlines looked for an updated DC-3 replacement to use on short-to-intermediate flights. The British built 163 copies of the portly twin-engine Vickers Viking, an unpressurized transport with 24 to 27 seats (later modified to carry 34 to 38 passengers) that cruised amiably at 320 km (200 miles) per hour over European routes and those of many Commonwealth countries. However, neither British, French, Italian, nor other European manufacturers enjoyed much success against American designs. For example, Consolidated Vultee Aircraft Corporation, more commonly known as Convair, built the speedy twin-engine 240/340/440 series, with trendy tricycle landing gear, which sold more than 1,000 models between 1947 and 1956, plus several hundred military versions that often trickled back into civil service. Convairs had a maximum cruising speed of 280 miles (450 km) per hour, and their pressurized cabins provided unaccustomed comfort for 40 to 50 passengers (depending on the model) in smaller airline markets around the world. Subsequent turboprop conversions kept the type in service for several decades.

During this period, the Soviet Union considered both practicality and politics for its extensive Aeroflot internal network. In the late 1930s, the country had acquired a state-of-the-art transport by signing a license agreement to build the Douglas DC-3, equipped with Soviet engines. Although numerous examples continued to serve in the postwar years, they were eventually succeeded by the Ilyushin Il-12, a trim unpressurized twin-engine transport that also featured retractable tricycle landing gear. A larger model, the Il-14, went into operation during the 1950s. Considered slow and technologically unsophisticated by modern standards, these planes played an ideological role in the Cold War by parrying Western imports. Production took place in communist-bloc countries; the Il-12 and Il-14 series numbered into the thousands, serving as military transports as well as the backbone for Aeroflot operations and civil duties in eastern Europe. They operated in China and were supplied to governments in Africa and Asia, where the Soviets wished to expand their influence.

The Il-12 and Il-14 transports had cruising speeds of about 320 km (200 miles) per hour and could carry 27 to 32 passengers over routes of up to 480 km (300 miles). Across the length and breadth of the Soviet Union, this seemingly modest performance served quite well. Every region of the country included cities and towns that often lacked both rail services and the benefits of all-weather roads. Rivers often offered a good alternative transport route, but long Russian winters and generally challenging conditions usually meant that they were frozen solid or characterized by seasonal floods and shifting navigational channels. Consequently, the schedules of Aeroflot—with its subsidized bargain-basement fares—constituted the only reasonably reliable transport and communication links throughout the year. Large long-range transports fulfilled the immediate—and crucial—need for timely, practical travel arrangements that bound thousands of large and small population centres to each other and to national passenger networks. The sturdy Il-12 and Il-14 transports could still be seen at airports through the 1980s.

After 1945, Douglas introduced its pressurized DC-6 to match the Lockheed Constellation on domestic and international routes. As they energetically courted sales to rival foreign airlines, American manufacturers constantly engaged in back-and-forth contests to improve their products. Since the North American market for airliners generated high-volume production, unit costs remained low, and they became highly competitive when priced against European transports. Eventually, the performance, quality, and value of postwar American designs led to their dominating presence in the airline fleets of major carriers overseas. Hoping to capture market share, Boeing utilized major components from the B-29 bomber and the C-97 cargo/tanker aircraft in building the Stratocruiser, a plane that offered unmatched luxury for air travelers in the late 1940s and early '50s. Its famously spacious cabin seated 55 passengers, and its bar/lounge, entered through a spiral staircase to the lower deck, created a sensation. Pan Am and British Overseas Airways Corporation (BOAC) quickly introduced Stratocruisers on premier routes across the North Atlantic. However, even the Stratocruiser faded against better, faster piston-engine airliners from Douglas and Lockheed.

But transcontinental schedules in the United States invariably included a stop for fuel en route; transatlantic flights between New York and Europe usually required refueling in Newfoundland, Iceland, or Ireland. These constraints began to evaporate in the 1950s with the Lockheed Super Constellation and the Douglas DC-7. The ultimate versions appeared in 1956–57 as the DC-7C, known as the "Seven Seas," which was capable of nonstop transatlantic flights in either direction, and the Lockheed 1649A Starliner, which could fly nonstop on polar routes from Los Angeles to Europe. The Starliner carried 75 passengers at speeds of 350 to 400 miles (560 to 640 km) per hour. Each of its Wright turbocompound radial engines developed 3,400 horsepower. Prior to the introduction of jet transports, these stalwart aircraft transformed the dynamics of air travel and continued in service with major airlines into the late 1960s.

Travel remained a stylish experience. Men donned coats and ties, and ladies appeared in hats and dresses. Airports featured first-class restaurants while airline cabin service featured crystal stemware and quality china. Until the 1950s, airline patrons characteristically traveled on a first-class basis, and fares remained relatively high until increased patronage paved the way for decreased prices. As early as 1953, domestic airlines in the United States reported more passenger miles than railroad Pullman travel. Before the end of the year, statistics revealed that airlines had also taken the lead as the prime mover for American travelers making trips of more that 200 miles (320 km). By 1958 the majority of U.S. passengers headed for Europe chose to go by plane rather than by ocean liner. Cabin-class seats proliferated on airliners, and fares dropped accordingly.

Even before the advent of jet airliners, piston-engine transports had usurped traditional railway and steamship technology as the principal mode of transport for long-distance trips. Domestically, convenient airline timetables enabled professional and collegiate sports teams to play tightly scheduled games on a nationwide basis. Airline business travel in the United States and overseas exploded. Piston-engine airliners made weekend ski trips and foreign excursions possible for thousands of middle-income individuals who could finally fit a 10-day European holiday into the time frame and budget of their annual vacation. As sociologist Max Lerner observed, postwar airways led to the democratization of American—and global—travel.

GENERAL AVIATION

Following World War I, a number of adventurous pilots began using airplanes for "utility aviation"—commercial photography, surveying, law enforcement, agricultural purposes such as seeding and crop dusting, and myriad other activities. In the United States, huge numbers of war-surplus engines and training aircraft, as well as larger planes such as the DH-4, offered a cheap and easy way to enter the flying business. Although barnstormers and acrobatic fliers all too often tarnished the image of aviation by performing foolhardy stunts in worn-out military castoffs, the phenomenon of utility aviation attracted increasing numbers of users. By the late 1920s, as the supply of war surplus aircraft and engines dried up, new companies began to offer improved engines and planes, including aircraft with enclosed cabins that could seat two to five people, bringing an end to open cockpits, helmets, goggles, and considerable engine noise.

Throughout the 1930s, despite the Great Depression, improvements continued, and the practice of using personal aircraft to conduct business became a recognized aspect of modern commerce, especially as American industry continued its pattern of geographic diversity and scattered divisions. In order to save time and expensive personnel costs, business aviation provided the means to deliver key people to locations where airlines did not fly and road or rail travel was indirect and time-consuming. Among the most popular private aircraft models were the two-seat Piper Cub, powered by a 65-horsepower engine that enabled a cruising speed of about 85 miles (140 km) per hour; the four-seat Cessna Airmaster, powered by a 145–165-horsepower engine that enabled a cruising speed of about 160 miles (260 km) per hour; and the seven to nine passenger Beechcraft Model 18, powered by two 450-horsepower engines that enabled a cruising speed of about 220 miles (350 km) per hour. Cessna and Beechcraft still used radial-piston engines, but Piper relied on a horizontally opposed four-cylinder engine that allowed

The Cessna Aircraft Company produced some 180 Airmasters between 1934 and 1941. The planes were especially popular for use in aerial photography because of their great stability in flight. Encyclopædia Britannica, Inc.

engineers to design a more streamlined engine nacelle. This type of engine became the preferred style for modern light-plane designs.

Other developments included Igor Sikorsky's work on practical piston-engine helicopters. Technological precedents in the 1930s included the autogiro, which used an

unpowered rotor for lift and a piston engine with propeller for forward flight, but they could not match the helicopter's ability for vertical flight and hovering. Postwar efforts to fly helicopters as short-haul passenger transports foundered, although they became invaluable in specialized missions (medevac, police patrol, traffic monitoring) and in sundry utility roles. However, compared with fixed-wing aircraft, their numbers remained small.

After World War II, the accelerating demand for personal and utility aircraft gave rise to the term *general aviation* to describe all flying that did not fall into the category of military or scheduled air transport. Manufacturers such as Piper, Cessna, and Beechcraft represented an expanding "light plane industry," although the general aviation sector included a host of modified aircraft that ranged from war surplus twin-engine Douglas A-26 bombers (rebuilt with luxury passenger cabins as fast, corporate transports) to four-engine DC-4 transports (reequipped with big internal fuselage tanks to dump retardants on forest fires). For the light plane builders, engine manufacturers such as Lycoming, Continental, and others perfected efficient horizontally opposed piston engines that produced from 65 to more than 200 horsepower;

mass production made them dominant in international applications; several appeared as turbo-supercharged designs delivering more than 300 horsepower.

Various engines powered a bewildering variety of postwar light planes, although Piper, Cessna, and Beechcraft led the market. Through the 1950s, Piper and Cessna marketed high-wing monoplanes with two to four seats, suitable for short-range personal business flying. Beechcraft introduced the stylish all-metal V-tailed Bonanza, with retractable landing gear, higher speed, and a roomy four-place cabin. Manufacturers installed a new generation of compact lightweight radio communication and navigational equipment (eventually dubbed avionics) that improved options to fly during bad weather. Eventually, all three manufacturers produced twin-engine aircraft, aimed at business travel, that could carry four to six people in more comfort at faster speeds. These designs eventually progressed into "cabin-class" corporate transports with supercharged engines, flown by a pilot and copilot, luxury accommodations for four to eight passengers in a pressurized cabin, a lavatory, and a door with a built-in stairway.

Although aircraft produced in the United States dominated the worldwide general aviation fleet, designs from other countries also won a significant market and became essential cogs in the economies of numerous global regions. Canada, with a long history of aircraft used in wilderness flying, produced a rugged example known as the Beaver, built by De Havilland's Canadian firm. With a big radial engine of 450 horsepower (or more), the high-wing Beaver could carry six to seven people (often more), or about 770 kg (1,700 pounds) of payload (usually more). The Beaver's moderate size allowed pilots to maneuver the plane in and out of primitive abbreviated airstrips. Fitted with either floats or skis, depending on the locale and season, Beavers could reach virtually any point in Canada's wilderness of forests, lakes, and Arctic terrain. De Havilland built 1,692 of these remarkably adaptable aircraft, and they served in 63 countries, ranging from tropical climes to polar regions.

The Soviet Union produced an aircraft of similar versatility, the Antonov AN-2. With its 1,000-horsepower radial engine, the AN-2 possessed a capacious barrel-like fuselage that could accommodate a dozen or so passengers or 1,800 kg (4,000 pounds) of cargo. Introduced in 1947, it featured a biplane configuration, and its large wing area gave it excellent flying characteristics for low-level agricultural applications—its principal intended function. But the AN-2's ability to operate from the isolated and rugged airstrips that dotted the Soviet Union made it a classic all-purpose airplane. In many remote areas such as Siberia, the AN-2 flew Aeroflot's colours as a local and short-haul passenger transport as well as cargo hauler and air ambulance. With more than 5,000 produced in Ukraine by the late 1950s, followed by approximately 11,900 in Poland during the 1960s, the AN-2 not only served throughout the Soviet bloc but also appeared in Africa, Latin America, and Asia. Within the Soviet bloc, Poland, Romania, and Czechoslovakia built a variety of other general aviation types, including agricultural models.

In Great Britain, Beagle Aircraft, Ltd., enjoyed some success in the 1960s. The distinctive name represented an acronym derived from British Executive and General Aviation Limited. Although several dozen airplanes entered service, they could not compete with their well-equipped counterparts from American manufacturers, whose products were backed by efficient international dealer networks. Other companies that produced planes for corporate use and small "feeder" airlines fared better. The twin-engine De Havilland (later, Hawker Siddeley) Dove arrived in 1945 as a low-wing design with retractable gear and a capacity for 11 passengers. It remained in production through the 1960s, with 554 Doves built, including 200 for military operators. The second aircraft was the Britten-Norman Islander, with headquarters located on the Isle of Wight. Designed as an up-to-date replacement for obsolete types such as the Dove, the twin-engine Islander debuted in the mid-1960s. Along with modern avionics, it featured a high wing and fixed gear, and its metal construction followed simple, easily fabricated lines with seats for nine passengers, keeping its cost to about one-third that of the Dove and similar planes. The Islander sold well, although its production sites tended to hopscotch around the world, including fabrication sites in Romania as well as the Philippines. Further modifications to the original design involved a remarkable stretch of the fuselage to accommodate the pilot and one passenger on the flight deck and 16 passengers in the main cabin and a redesigned wing and tail assembly. With its highly distinctive third piston engine mounted atop the vertical tail rudder, it became the Tri-Islander. Still flying in the 21st century, the various Islanders served effectively in many thinly populated areas having geographical constraints, such as the Caribbean, and carried thousands of passengers there and elsewhere around the world.

The French were also busy producing light planes to compete with American products. As in Britain, dozens of types came and went during the postwar decades. Among those with staying power, factory-built aircraft designed for sale in kit form enjoyed lively sales, although many of them remained partially completed and moldering away in basements, garages, and barns. In 1966 an extensive realignment of French manufacturers led to the formation of Société de Construction d'Avions de Tourisme et d'Affaires, or Socata. The new company continued to build the proven Rallye, a trim two-passenger monoplane, but achieved notable success with its own range of larger, more powerful single-engine business planes with retractable gear. By the 1990s, the performance and reliability of the Socata Tobago and Trinidad series had made them serious competitors in the North American market.

Through the 1960s, piston-engine airliners still played a major role in air travel, and their ubiquitous counterparts in general aviation enlivened the aeronautical scene. In 1969 commercial airlines counted about 2,500 transports; 122,500 aircraft represented the general aviation fleet. The subsequent impact of gas-turbine engines transformed both categories. Older piston-engine airliners often soldiered on as firefighting tankers, while many others shuttled passengers and cargo from remote airfields to various destinations. Myriads of piston-powered light planes continue to populate the airways everywhere. The grand epoch of piston-engine aircraft may have waned, but their story continues.

CHAPTER 5

THE JET AGE

From the very invention of flight at the beginning of the 20th century, military aircraft and engines generally led the way, and commercial aviation followed. At first this was also the case in the jet age, which began with the invention of jet engines under military sponsorship in the 1930s and '40s. By the late 20th century, however, commercial jet-engine technology had come to rival and sometimes even lead military technology in several areas of engine design. And, although it was not immediately evident, the invention of the jet engine had a far more significant social effect on the world through commercial aviation than through its military counterpart. Commercial jet aircraft have revolutionized world travel, opening up every corner of the world not just to the affluent but to the ordinary citizens of many countries.

FIRST EXPERIMENTS

Just as George Cayley and John Stringfellow of England, Lawrence Hargrave of Australia, Otto Lilienthal of Germany, and others had conducted experiments with flight in the years preceding Wilbur and Orville Wright's successful Wright flyer of 1903, so, too, were there many pioneers in the field of turbine engines before the almost simultaneous inventive successes of Frank Whittle of England and Hans von Ohain of Germany in the 1930s and '40s.

The early experimenters included the inventor Heron of Alexandria (*c.* 50 CE), with his steam-powered aeolipile. In about 1500, Leonardo da Vinci created a sketch of a chimney jack that used hot gases flowing up a chimney to drive fanlike blades that in turn rotated a spit. Both the aeolipile and the spit operated on principles first explained in 1687 by Isaac Newton, whose laws of motion formed the basis for modern propulsion theory. By 1872 German engineer Franz Stolze had designed the first true gas-turbine engine.

In the United States, Sanford A. Moss, an engineer with the General Electric Co., came close to inventing a jet engine in 1918 with his turbosupercharger, which used hot gases from the engine exhaust to drive a turbine that in turn drove a centrifugal compressor to supercharge the engine. (The invention was vital to American air power during World War II.) The process was carried a step further in 1920, when Alan A. Griffith of England developed a theory of turbine design based on gas flow past airfoils rather than through passages. Griffith subsequently worked for many years for Rolls-Royce, Ltd.

WORLD WAR II

The jet engine was unusual in that it was independently brought to fruition at about the same time in two countries that would soon again be at war. In Great Britain, a Royal Air Force officer, Frank Whittle, invented the gas-turbine engine that would power the first British jet, the Gloster E.28/39, which made its first flight on May 15, 1941. In Germany, Hans Joachim Pabst von Ohain worked on the problem of gas-turbine engines without any knowledge of Whittle's efforts. Von Ohain found backing from the aviation industrialist Ernst Heinkel, who sought to have an engine-manufacturing capability to complement his aircraft company. Work proceeded swiftly, and on Aug. 27, 1939, von Ohain's HeS.3B engine enabled Erich Warsitz to make the world's first successful turbojet-powered flight in history in the Heinkel He 178.

Notable American experimenters in jet-aviation technology include Nathan Price of Lockheed Corporation, who designed and built the L-1000, and Vladimir Pavlecki and Art Phelan at Northrop Aircraft, Inc.

Britain's initial setbacks during World War II spurred interest in developing the jet engine, while Germany's successes led its leaders to a decision to defer all technical developments in weaponry that could not be realized within a year. Despite this, the Junkers Motorenwerke GmbH had assigned Anselm Franz to develop a jet engine, beginning in 1940. Junkers put his engine into production, and it powered the first operational jet fighter in history, the German Messerschmitt Me 262.

Britain and the United States also introduced jet fighters, with the British Gloster Meteor making its first flight on March 5, 1943. The first American jet fighter, the Bell P-59A, lacked the performance necessary for combat, so the first operational U.S. jet fighter was the Lockheed P-80A, which arrived too late for combat in World War II. It would prove to be invaluable during the Korean War just five years later, though. The Soviet Union also conducted experiments with jet engines, including the installation of ramjets, but these were on a small scale.

TECHNICAL ADVANTAGES AND CHALLENGES

Whittle, von Ohain, and others met resistance to their ideas because conventional thinkers believed that the jet engine would produce too little power and consume too much fuel to be economically practical. It was not generally recognized that at higher altitudes the jet would produce more power with acceptable fuel efficiency. Understandably, even the most dedicated engine experts did not anticipate the rapid pace at which jet-engine performance would be improved.

It happened that the jet engine entered the propulsion scene at a time when conventional reciprocating engines and propellers were reaching their physical limits. Propellers were already encountering supersonic tip-speeds that destroyed their efficiency, and engines had grown so complex that additional horsepower in the 3,000–4,000 range depended on a large number of cylinders and complex supercharging that generated problems in operation and maintenance.

With their continuous rotary motion, jet engines were mechanically simpler and smoother than reciprocating pistons with their rough pounding. Jet engines developed rapidly and by 1950 had reached levels of power that were impossible with piston engines. Reciprocating engines for aircraft had reached a practical limit with the 3,500-horsepower, 28-cylinder Pratt & Whitney R-4360 engine, while some modern jet engines, such as the General Electric GE90-115, can produce as much as 115,000 pounds of thrust. The R-4360 engines powered the last generation of piston-powered bombers—namely, the Boeing B-50, which was in frontline service for only a few years as a bomber before being relegated to a (jet-assisted) tanker role. In contrast, the Boeing 777, which uses the GE90-115 engine, first flew in 2003 and will likely remain in service for two or more decades. Thrust and horsepower are difficult to equate, but one pound of thrust is equivalent to one horsepower at 375 miles (600 km) per hour.

It was not immediately obvious that the jet engine required major advances in airframe design and support

THE BLACK BOX

The black box, or flight recorder, is an instrument that records the performance and condition of an aircraft in flight. Governmental regulatory agencies require these devices on commercial aircraft to make possible the analysis of crashes or other unusual occurrences. Flight recorders actually consist of two functional devices, the flight data recorder (FDR) and the cockpit voice recorder (CVR), though sometimes these two devices are packaged together in one combined unit. The FDR records many variables, not only basic aircraft conditions such as airspeed, altitude, heading, vertical acceleration, and pitch but hundreds of individual instrument readings and internal environmental conditions. The CVR records verbal communication between crew members within the aircraft's cockpit as well as voice transmissions by radio. Aircraft sounds audible in the cockpit are also caught on the recorder. Flight recorders are commonly carried in the tail of the aircraft, which is usually the structure that is subject to the least impact in the event of a crash. In spite of the popular name *black box*, flight recorders are painted a highly visible vermilion colour known as "international orange."

The voice and instrument data processed by the flight recorder are stored in digital format on solid-state memory boards. Up to two hours of cockpit sound and 25 hours of flight data are stored, new data continuously replacing the old. The memory boards are housed within a box or cylinder called the crash-survivable memory unit. This is the only truly survivable component of the flight recorder (the other components, such as the data processor, are not necessary for retrieval of data). Consisting of a heavy stainless-steel shell wrapped within layers of insulating material and covered by an aluminum housing, a memory unit is expected to survive impacts of 3,400 G's, flame temperatures as high as 1,100 °C (2,000 °F), and pressures encountered at 6,000 metres (20,000 feet) underwater. In the event of a crash at sea, flight recorders are equipped with a sonar device that is designed to emit an ultrasonic locator signal for at least 30 days.

Flight recorders of varying levels of sophistication have been in existence almost since the beginning of manned flight. The Wright brothers are said to have installed a device on their first flyer of 1903 that logged such parameters as propeller rotation and airspeed, and Charles Lindbergh, in his epoch-making flight across the Atlantic in

1927, employed a barometric device that sensed changes in air pressure (and therefore altitude) and recorded these changes by tracing lines on a rotating spool.

As civil aviation developed in the years before World War II, "crash-survivable" flight recorders came to be seen as a valuable tool in analyzing aviation disasters and contributing to the design of safer aircraft. However, truly serviceable recorders that had any chance of surviving plane crashes were not produced until several years after the war. In the United States, credit for the first survivable FDR is given to James J. Ryan, an engineer employed by General Mills in the early 1950s. Ryan's VGA Flight Recorder sensed changes in velocity (V), gravitational forces (G), and altitude (A) and inscribed the measurements on a slowly moving strip of aluminum foil. As released in 1953 and sold by General Mills to the Lockheed Aircraft Company, the entire apparatus was enclosed in a yellow-painted spherical shell. Beginning in 1958, larger civilian passenger aircraft in the United States were required to carry survivable FDRs, and numerous other devices were produced employing various recording media, from metal strips to, eventually, magnetic tape.

Parallel developments occurred elsewhere in the world. A series of disastrous crashes of De Havilland Comet jetliners in 1953–54 spurred David Warren, a scientist at Australia's Aeronautical Research Laboratory (ARL), to design the first combined FDR and CVR. The recording medium for Warren's ARL Flight Memory Unit was steel wire of the type then being used in magnetic audio recorders. After a demonstration of the device in Britain in 1958, a journalist is said to have given it the sobriquet *black box* (the common name for all flight recorders to this day), though Warren's recorder, as produced commercially by S. Davall & Son beginning in 1960, was housed in an egg-shaped casing that was painted red. Other theories of the origin of the term *black box* have been offered, including the charred appearance of early flight recorders retrieved from a fiery crash.

During the 1960s, crash-protected FDRs and CVRs became mandatory on airliners around the world. Most flight recorders employed magnetic tape, but during the 1990s a great advancement came with the advent of solid-state memory devices. Memory boards are more survivable than recording tape, and the data stored on them can be retrieved quickly by a computer carrying the proper software. A complete picture can be created of conditions on the aircraft during the recorded period, including a computer-animated diagram of the aircraft's positions and movements. Verbal exchanges and cockpit sounds retrieved from CVR data are transcribed into documents that are made available to investigators along with the actual recordings. The release of these materials to the public is strictly regulated.

facilities. First, airframes needed to be much larger to carry the additional passengers required to make jet aircraft economically sound. They would also have to be much stronger to accommodate the pressurized fuselage and the many transitions between low altitudes for take-offs and landings and high altitudes for cruising. Another structural change was to sweep the wings back to reduce the drag increase associated with approaching supersonic flight. This was a possibility first elucidated by German engineer Adolph Buseman in 1935 and a few years later independently by Robert T. Jones at the U.S. National Advisory Committee for Aeronautics (NACA). In addition, aircraft and ground instrumentation became far more sophisticated. Ground handling equipment to service the aircraft also was vastly improved, as was airport infrastructure for refueling, loading, and unloading. Navigation and en-route surveillance were also much improved to handle the initial growth of jet traffic but subsequently had to be overhauled again when the number of flights grew to the point of saturating air traffic control capability.

It was recognized almost from the start that the higher construction cost of the jet airliner would need to be amortized through intensive use. What was not initially known, though, was the greater longevity that jet airliners would have compared with their piston-engine predecessors. The improvement in engine operation has been the most spectacular, with jet engines now having intervals between overhauls that run into tens of thousands of hours and with corrosion and molecular decay rather than wear being the biggest maintenance problem.

While advances in jet aviation have been phenomenal, the industry faces greater risks than ever before. The growth in performance has been matched by a growth in cost and a diminution of the number of aircraft required by civil and military customers. Commercial airliners are more cost effective than ever before and last longer. And development of new aircraft costs billions of dollars, requiring a continued growth in passenger traffic to keep production levels steady or climbing.

THE AIRLINES RE-EQUIP

In Britain, the production of advanced commercial aircraft had been abandoned during the war, while the greater capacity and efficiency of American industry allowed the creation of the long-distance piston-engine Douglas C-54 (DC-4) and Lockheed C-69 Constellation aircraft. A committee headed by aviation pioneer and former member of Parliament John Moore-Brabazon was established in 1943 to discuss postwar prospects of reviving the British air-transport industry, and among the suggestions was a specification for a transatlantic mailplane. De Havilland began design studies that led to the first flight of the D.H. 106 Comet jet airliner on July 27, 1949. Britain had stolen a march on the world, for the 36-seat Comet could fly at 800 km (500 miles) per hour for up to 2,400 km (1,500 miles).

Boeing, Douglas, and Lockheed were stunned; though the Comet was considered too small and too short-ranged for American airline routes, they could offer no jet competitor. Britain's great lead went down in flames, however, when several Comets crashed, which led to its withdrawal from service in 1954. The later crashes were ultimately attributed to structural failure of the pressure cabin because of metal fatigue.

Boeing made a great advance with its revolutionary B-47 bomber, first flown on Dec. 17, 1947. The six-engine, swept-wing aircraft was purchased in large quantities (2,032) by the U.S. Air Force. This gave Boeing the engineering and financial basis to create the Model 367-80, a prototype for both the later 707 passenger plane and the KC-135 tanker. Although a tremendous gamble for Boeing, which for many years had been almost entirely a military supplier, the 707 was a commercial success after entering service in 1958. Douglas responded with its similar looking DC-8. Both aircraft were larger (some configurations could carry more than 200 passengers) and faster (more than 600 miles [1,000 km] per hour) than the modified Comet 4 that began service on the New York to London route on Oct. 4, 1958.

Boeing and Douglas quickly dominated the market, making it difficult for a later entry, the CV-880, from Consolidated Vultee Aircraft Corporation, more commonly known as Convair, to gain a foothold. Convair had stressed speed rather than passenger capacity, but the 880 and the improved 990 that followed it were commercial disasters that almost forced the company out of business.

Britain tried desperately to regain its footing in the airliner market but found that its Commonwealth route structures required specialized aircraft designs that were not competitive with the Boeing and Douglas products in the world market. The British had their greatest success with turboprop airliners, in which the propulsive power of the jet engines was transferred to a propeller through a gear box. The most prominent of these was the Vickers

Viscount, which was built in larger numbers (444) than any other British airliner. The Viscount could carry from 40 to 65 passengers at a cruising speed of 570 to 590 km (355 to 365 miles) per hour, depending on configuration. It was employed most extensively by British European Airways. Other British jet airliners, such as the British Aircraft Corporation (BAC) One-Eleven, the Vickers VC-10, and the Hawker Siddeley Aviation Trident, were produced in relatively small numbers and were not outstanding commercial successes because of the superb production and marketing of equivalent U.S. airliners.

France succeeded with its first effort at a jet airliner, creating the Sud-Est (later Aérospatiale) SE 210 Caravelle, a medium-range turbojet intended primarily for the continental European market. First flown on May 27, 1955, the Caravelle achieved sales of 282 aircraft, and a turbofan-powered variant was used for domestic routes by airlines in the United States—a marketing coup at the time. The Caravelle was the world's first airliner to have rear-mounted engines, a design feature that was adopted for some uses by all other major manufacturers.

Jet airliners were a genuine requirement for the Soviet Union because of its vast expanse of territory, which included 10 time zones. The Tupolev Tu-104 prototype made its first flight on June 17, 1955, only 11 months after the first flight of the Boeing 367–80 but 30 months before the first flight of a production 707. Tupolev had leaped ahead by using the components of the Tu-16 bomber, adding only a new 55-seat pressurized fuselage. The Tu-104 served well and reliably for many years but would not have been considered for use by Western airlines because of its high operating costs. It began a dynasty of Tupolev airliners that continues to this day.

Tupolev's efforts were complemented by those of Ilyushin, which has produced a long series of successful turboprop and jet airliners that in recent years have benefited by access to Western engines and electronics technology. After the collapse of the Soviet Union on Dec. 25, 1991, the great Soviet airline Aeroflot was broken up, and former satellite countries began to look to the West for airliners that were more economical to operate. The result was an immense reduction in both development and production of Russian airliners and an utter inability to compete with Western airliner builders.

PROGRESS IN ENGINES AND AIRFRAMES

Two stages in the jetliner's development marked the 1960s. The first was the adoption of the turbofan engine. The turbofan gains economy by having much of its thrust pass around the engine core rather than through it. The second stage was marked by the introduction of the wide-bodied, 400-seat Boeing 747 in 1969. This large, swift, and long-ranged aircraft created a transportation revolution. Whereas air travel had once been confined to the affluent, it now became a mass-market conveyance as airline ticket prices fell and airlines became more sophisticated in their pricing practices. As the total market grew, smaller jet and turboprop airliners were developed for shorter routes.

Boeing had already demonstrated its mastery of the technique of creating aircraft to meet new demands by creating first the three-engine T-tailed 727 in 1963, followed by a succession of aircraft (the 737 [1967], 757 [1982], 767 [1981], 777 [2003], and 787 [2007]) that were tailored to the needs of specific airlines and routes. (The 737, with more than 6,000 sales, is the most produced jet transport in history.) Each of these models was modified and improved over time to take advantage of technical developments,

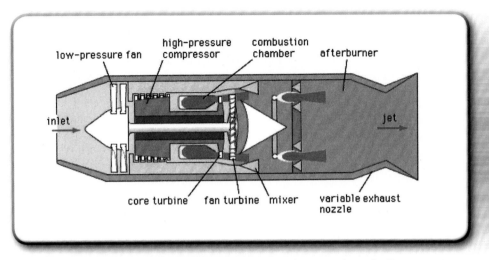

Low-bypass turbofan with afterburner. Copyright Encyclopædia Britannica, Inc.; rendering for this edition by Rosen Educational Services

and, as a result, Boeing had an excellent portfolio of aircraft to offer airline companies.

During the period of Boeing's expansion, Douglas ran into management problems, and while its DC-9 was a spectacular success, it could not match Boeing's proliferation of designs. Douglas was acquired by McDonnell Aircraft Corporation in 1967, forming McDonnell Douglas Corporation, and the McDonnell Douglas DC-10 was created to meet an estimated market requirement for about 750 wide-bodied aircraft. Lockheed sought to enter the same market with its technologically more advanced L-1011 TriStar. McDonnell Douglas sold 446 DC-10s, while Lockheed sold 250 TriStars, with both companies losing massive amounts of money. McDonnell Douglas belatedly struggled on with the MD-11, an improved DC-10, while continuing the DC-9 as the MD-80 and MD-90 series. When Boeing acquired the firm in 1997, it applied the designation 717 to one version of the twin-engine jet.

In spite of the intense nature of the competition to build jet airliners, a new entrant appeared in the early 1970s following intense industrial and political negotiations. Airbus Industrie was co-owned by French, German, British, Spanish, Dutch, and Belgium companies and sub-contracted many parts to still other countries. Established in December 1970 to build the Airbus A300 wide-bodied twin, the company was discounted at first as having little chance to compete. However, its aircraft were widely accepted, and a series of designs followed that established a family of aircraft that matched Boeing's offerings—and, with the introduction of the A380 in 2005, threatened to exceed them. The Airbus family marched steadily forward in size, number, and utility until it consisted of no fewer than 14 different series of aircraft. Complaints from the United States that Airbus was being subsidized by the various European governments was countered by the charge that American manufacturers were in effect subsidized by their sale of aircraft to the U.S. military and by National Aeronautics and Space Administration (NASA) research.

As the jet engine matured, it moved successively to other segments of the airline market and then, as turbo-shafts and turboprops, respectively, into helicopters and business aircraft. The success of the Viscount turboprop airliner was emulated by a host of others. Relatively small airlines, using these planes for routes connecting smaller cities, became associated with the larger carriers and often adopted the same name. In the late 1990s, smaller jets with room for 50 to 90 passengers began to replace the turboprops. This trend was part of a dramatic make-over in the profile and operations of airlines, especially in North America.

Among business aircraft, smaller jet engines, with good fuel-consumption characteristics, became available to power executive jets. The first to appear included the

Executive jets have become more common since the 1960s. Encyclopædia Britannica, Inc.

Lockheed JetStar of 1957, which was soon followed by the North American Sabreliner. These aircraft were eclipsed by the appearance in 1963 of the Learjet 23. This five-to-seven-passenger jet had a top speed of about 560 miles (900 km) per hour and a range of 1,830 miles (2,945 km). Favoured by celebrities, *Learjet* became almost a generic term for the many executive jets that followed. Powered by turbofans, these included excellent aircraft from France (Dassault), Israel (IAI), and the United Kingdom (De Havilland and Hawker Siddeley).

Businesses had used aircraft since the early 1920s, and a substantial fleet of twin piston-engine executive aircraft existed when the executive jets arrived. Although companies were loath to admit it, most executive jets were initially purchased as a perquisite of the top management, usually for a chief executive officer who liked to fly and found the executive jet's performance comparable to that of airliners. In time, however, it was realized that executive

AIR FORCE ONE

Any aircraft of the U.S. Air Force that is carrying the president of the United States is called Air Force One. Strictly speaking, Air Force One is the radio call sign adopted by any Air Force plane while the president is aboard. In common parlance, however, the call sign has become identified with specific aircraft reserved for use by the president for travel within the United States or abroad. Since 1991 two such aircraft have been in service: identical Boeing 747-200B jumbo jets bearing the tail numbers 28000 and 29000 and the Air Force designation VC-25A.

Each of the current Air Force One aircraft is equipped with classified security and defense systems, including measures to protect onboard electronics against the electromagnetic pulse of a nuclear explosion. A telecommunications centre is located in the upper level, and in the lower level is a cargo hold with a self-contained baggage-handling system. The middle level contains accommodations for as many as 70 passengers in addition to the crew of 26. These accommodations include seating and work areas for media representatives,

Air Force One, a Boeing 747 reserved for use by the president of the United States, flying over Mount Rushmore, South Dakota. U.S. Air Force

security staff, and other personnel; a combination conference-dining room; an in-flight pharmacy and emergency medical equipment; and two galleys in which as many as 100 servings per meal can be prepared. The presidential suite, located in the quiet forward area of the plane, contains an office, a bedroom, and a lavatory. The two Air Force One jets have a range of almost 8,000 miles (more than 12,000 km) unrefueled, but with in-flight refueling they are capable of circling the globe.

The first American president to fly while in office was Franklin D. Roosevelt, and all presidents since Roosevelt have had their own reserved aircraft. At first these were propeller-driven planes (usually adapted from military transports), but starting with Pres. Dwight D. Eisenhower jets entered the presidential fleet. According to popular lore, the call sign Air Force One was first invoked by the pilot of one of Eisenhower's planes during a flight to Florida, when he was concerned that air traffic controllers might confuse the presidential plane's call sign, Air Force 610, with a similar call sign of a nearby commercial airliner. In 1962, during the administration of John F. Kennedy, the first jet specifically built for presidential use was delivered—a Boeing 707, given the tail number 26000 and the official designation VC-137C. This jet was destined to become a symbol of the power and prestige of the U.S. presidency and to create in the public imagination the very idea of Air Force One. Industrial designer Raymond Loewy contributed a distinctive blue-and-white colour scheme to the exterior as well as a logo that featured the title "United States of America" on the fuselage, the U.S. flag on the tail, and the presidential seal on both sides of the nose. This design has been carried over to all subsequent Air Force One planes.

In June 1963 the new jet carried Kennedy to a divided Berlin, where he issued his famous declaration "Ich bin ein Berliner," and in November 1963 it transported the assassinated president back to Washington from Dallas. Lyndon B. Johnson was sworn in as president on the plane, and it continued to serve as the primary or backup Air Force One during the administrations of Johnson, Richard M. Nixon, Gerald R. Ford, Jimmy Carter, Ronald Reagan, and George H.W. Bush. In 1972 the plane was joined by a sister aircraft, given the tail number 27000; this was the plane that flew Nixon back to private life in California upon his sudden resignation in August 1974. Both planes went through several refittings before being replaced for duty as Air Force One in 1990–91 by the current pair of 747s. Aircraft 26000 was retired from the presidential fleet in 1998 at Wright-Patterson Air Force Base, Dayton, Ohio, where it is on display at the National Museum of the United States Air Force, and 27000 was retired in 2001 and is now on display at the Ronald W. Reagan Presidential Library and Museum in Simi Valley, Calif.

The current Air Force One jets are based at Andrews Air Force Base in Maryland, near Washington, D.C., and are assigned to the 89th Airlift Wing of the Air Force's Air Mobility Command. They have served presidents, vice presidents (at which time they are known as Air Force Two), and other dignitaries under the administrations of George H.W. Bush, Bill Clinton, George W. Bush, and Barack Obama. The pair of jets is slated for replacement by three new aircraft between 2017 and 2021.

aircraft were tools in exactly the same way that factory machines or computers were tools, and they were subsequently purchased in far larger numbers on that basis. The top executive jets, including the Boeing Business Jet (a variation of the 737), the Bombardier Global Express, the Dassault Falcon 900, and the Gulfstream 500/550, featured intercontinental range and high subsonic speeds.

AVIONICS, PASSENGER SUPPORT, AND SAFETY

During the jet age, *avionics*, a coined term meaning "aviation electronics," has seen a rapid growth in every aspect, including navigation, instrumentation, communication, safety, and landing assistance.

The advent of the cathode-ray oscilloscope and its application to aircraft spurred the avionics revolution, which had begun with relatively primitive radios. While the initial uses of the cathode-ray display were for military purposes (detecting incoming enemy aircraft), it was soon applied to in-flight navigation, controlling aircraft in terminal areas, and landing operations. The ground-controlled approach (GCA), in which a ground observer monitors the course and descent angle of an aircraft via radar, enables pilots to land under extremely adverse weather conditions. GCA was used extensively by the U.S. military during the 1948 Berlin blockade and airlift and was approved for U.S. civil airline use in 1949. Another avionics system, the instrument landing system (ILS), uses onboard instruments to interpret signals sent from ground stations. A rather primitive ILS was introduced in 1929 but became truly useful only after 1945. As radar became more powerful and available in greater quantity, it became useful for monitoring aircraft as they progressed along their routes.

In communications, radios operating in very high frequency (VHF) reappeared after World War II and became standard for civil and commercial aircraft, while military aircraft adopted ultrahigh frequency (UHF). The introduction of satellite communication in the early 1960s, while initially expensive, finally offered the potential to achieve real-time surveillance of every airborne aircraft anywhere in the world. Meanwhile, the use of satellites for navigation leaped forward in the mid-1990s, in part because its adoption was less expensive than satellite communications and in part because of its pinpoint accuracy. Global positioning system (GPS) satellites can be expected to eventually be used for terminal control and landing approaches.

The cathode-ray display also found its way into the cockpit, where it replaced standard analog information presentations and made far more information instantly available to pilots. When integrated into automatic pilots, these displays make cockpit resource management a key element of flying safety. There were almost-continuous experiments with the cathode-ray tube from the mid-1970s, but it was supplanted by the computer-based electronic display in the 1980s. The first true "glass cockpit" was found in the Boeing 767 (1981). Since that time, electronic displays have progressed throughout aviation and may now be found even in light aircraft. The next generation in cockpit management is the Multifunction Electronic Display Subsystem (MEDS), which allows pilots to call up desired information on a liquid crystal display (LCD). Besides being more easily understood by a computer-literate generation of pilots, MEDS is less expensive to maintain and more easily updated than conventional instrumentation.

In the area of passenger support, the jet age excelled in the ticketing process and in the creation of large terminals, but in the view of many experienced travelers it regressed in the area of onboard comfort. Seating became more restricted, and the rapid retrieval of baggage seemed to remain an unsolvable problem. To some extent, onboard electronics compensated for these inconveniences by providing amenities such as telephones, television, and the Internet. Most travelers, however, would settle for a little more hip and leg room. Safety is one area in which there has been continual progress, with military and commercial aviation having vastly improved their safety records by any measure.

SUPERSONIC FLIGHT

Supersonic flight is passage through the air at speed greater than the local velocity of sound. The speed of sound (Mach 1) varies with atmospheric pressure and temperature: in air at a temperature of 15 °C (59 °F) and sea-level pressure, sound travels at about 1,225 km (760 miles) per hour. At speeds beyond about five times the velocity of sound (Mach 5), the term *hypersonic flight* is employed. An object traveling through the Earth's atmosphere at supersonic speed generates a sonic boom—i.e., a shock wave heard on the ground as a sound like a loud explosion.

The first aircraft to fly at supersonic speeds was a Bell XS-1 rocket-powered research plane piloted by Major Charles E. Yeager of the U.S. Air Force on Oct. 14, 1947. After being dropped from the belly of a Boeing B-29 mother ship, the XS-1 broke the (local) sound barrier at 1,066 km (662 miles) per hour and attained a top speed of 1,126 km (700 miles) per hour, or Mach 1.06. Thereafter many military aircraft capable of supersonic flight were built, though their speed was generally limited to Mach 2.5 because of problems caused by frictional heating of the skin of the plane.

The first supersonic passenger-carrying commercial airplane (or supersonic transport, SST), the Concorde, was built jointly by Aérospatiale and British Aerospace. The Concorde had a maximum cruising speed of 2,179 km (1,354 miles) per hour, or Mach 2.04. This beautiful airliner, the first example of which flew on March 2, 1969, made its first transatlantic crossing on Sept. 26, 1973, and entered regular service in 1976. The aircraft proved a technical miracle but an economic disaster, however. Never financially profitable, it was retired in 2003.

The only other SST to see service was the Tupolev design bureau's Tu-144. The prototype of this Soviet SST made its first flight on Dec. 31, 1968, and was so similar in appearance and performance to the more highly publicized Anglo-French plane that it was called the "Concordski." In its production model the Tu-144 was 65.7 metres (215.6

THE CONCORDE

On Jan. 21, 1976, the Anglo-French Concorde inaugurated the world's first scheduled supersonic passenger service. British Airways initially flew the aircraft from London to Bahrain, and Air France flew it from Paris to Rio de Janeiro. Both airlines added regular service to Washington, D.C., in May 1976 and to New York City in November 1977. Other routes were added temporarily or seasonally, and the Concorde was flown on chartered flights to destinations all over the world.

The Concorde was the first major cooperative venture of European countries to design and build an aircraft. On Nov. 29, 1962, Britain and France signed a treaty to share costs and risks in producing an SST. British Aerospace and the French firm Aérospatiale were responsible for the airframe, while Britain's Rolls-Royce and France's SNECMA (Société Nationale d'Étude et de Construction de Moteurs d'Aviation) developed the jet engines. The result was a technological masterpiece that made its first flight on March 2, 1969. The Concorde's maximum cruising speed Mach 2.04 (more than twice the speed of sound) allowed the aircraft to reduce the flight time between London and New York to about three hours. The Concorde proved that European governments and manufacturers could cooperate in complex ventures, and it helped to ensure that Europe would remain at the technical forefront of aerospace development.

However, the development costs of the Concorde were so great that they could never be recovered from operations, so, for reasons of national prestige, they were simply written off. In addition, the aircraft's noise and operating expense limited its service. Financial losses led both airlines to cut routes, eventually leaving New York City as their only regular destination. Concorde operations were finally ceased by Air France in May 2003 and by British Airways in October 2003. Only 14 of the aircraft actually went into service. One of them is on display at a special facility of the National Air and Space Museum at Washington Dulles International Airport in Virginia.

feet) in length, with a wingspan of 28.8 metres (94.5 feet). Its normal cruising speed was up to Mach 2.2, more than twice the speed of sound. Among its notable features were "double-delta" swept-back wings, "moustache" foreplanes that pivoted out from the fuselage just aft of the flight deck to improve flight characteristics during takeoff and landing, and a nose section that could be "drooped" downward to improve the crew's line of vision during takeoff and landing. The aircraft had an inauspicious start when the first production Tu-144 crashed at the 1973 Paris Air Show. The aircraft was put into commercial service on the Moscow–Alma Ata route, flying mail (1975) and then passengers (1978), but the planes were pulled from service following another crash in 1978. Later models continued to fly as test beds for the technology of supersonic flight.

CHAPTER 6

Helicopters, Hang Gliders, and Ultralights

I n addition to fixed-wing aircraft, flight is achieved by helicopters, hang gliders, and ultralights. Helicopters take to the air using the principles of vertical flight. Hang gliders employ kite-like wings for lift and are controlled by the shifting weight of the pilot's body. Ultralights are advanced craft made with lightweight materials and powered by small internal-combustion engines, electric motors fueled by solar cells, or human muscle alone.

THE HELICOPTER

Helicopters are equipped with one or more power-driven horizontal propellers or rotors that enable the craft to take off and land vertically, move in any direction, or remain stationary in the air.

The idea of taking off vertically, making the transition to horizontal flight to the destination, and landing vertically has been for centuries the dream of inventors. It is the most logical form of flight, dispensing as it does with large landing fields located far from city centres and the inevitable intervening modes of travel—automobile, subway, bus—that flight in conventional aircraft usually requires.

But vertical flight is also the most demanding challenge in flying, requiring more sophistication in structure, power, and control than conventional fixed-wing aircraft. These difficulties, solved over time by determined

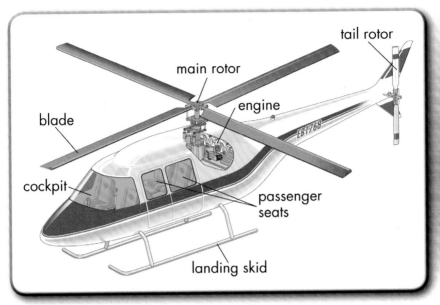

Components of a helicopter. Encyclopædia Britannica, Inc.

engineers and inventors, made the progress of vertical flight seem slow compared to that of conventional flight. The first useful helicopters did not appear until the early 1940s.

HISTORY

One important characteristic of the history of vertical flight is the pervasive human interest in the subject; inventors in many countries took up the challenge over the years, achieving varying degrees of success. The history of vertical flight began at least as early as about 400 CE; there are historical references to a Chinese kite that used a rotary wing as a source of lift. Toys using the principle of the helicopter—a rotary blade turned by the pull of a string—were known during the Middle Ages. During the latter part of the 15th century, Leonardo da Vinci made drawings of a helicopter that used a spiral airscrew to obtain lift. A toy helicopter, using rotors made out of the feathers of birds, was presented to the French Academy of Science in 1784 by two artisans, Launoy and Bienvenu; this toy forecast a more successful model created in 1870 by Alphonse Pénaud in France.

The first scientific exposition of the principles that ultimately led to the successful helicopter came in 1843 from Sir George Cayley, who is also regarded by many as the father of fixed-wing flight. From that point on, a veritable gene pool of helicopter ideas was spawned by numerous inventors, almost entirely in model or sketch form. Many were technical dead ends, but others contributed a portion of the ultimate solution. In 1907 there were two significant steps forward. On September 29, the Breguet brothers, Louis and Jacques, under the guidance of the physiologist and aviation pioneer Charles Richet made a short flight in their Gyroplane No. 1, powered by a 45-horsepower engine. The Gyroplane had a spiderweb-like frame and four sets of rotors. The piloted aircraft lifted from the ground to a height of about two feet, but it was tethered and not under any control. Breguet went on to become a famous name in French aviation, and in time Louis returned to successful work in helicopters. Later, in November, their countryman Paul Cornu, who was a bicycle maker like the Wright brothers, attained a free flight of about 20 seconds' duration, reaching a height of one foot in a twin-rotor craft powered by a 24-horsepower engine. Another man who, like the Breguets, would flirt with the helicopter, go on to make his name with fixed-wing aircraft, and then later return to the challenge of vertical flight, was Igor Sikorsky, who made some unsuccessful experiments at about the same time.

The next 25 years were characterized by two main trends in vertical flight. One was the wide spread of minor successes with helicopters; the second was the appearance and apparent success of the autogiro.

The helicopter saw incremental success in many countries, and the following short review will highlight only those whose contributions were ultimately found in successfully developed helicopters. In 1912 the Danish inventor Jacob Ellehammer made short hops in a helicopter that featured contrarotating rotors and cyclic pitch control, the latter an important insight into the problem of control. On Dec. 18, 1922, a complex helicopter designed by George de Bothezat for the U.S. Army Air Force lifted off the ground for slightly less than two minutes, under minimum control. In France on May 4, 1924, Étienne Oehmichen established a distance record for helicopters by flying a circle of a kilometre's length.

In Spain in the previous year, on Jan. 9, 1923, Juan de la Cierva made the first successful flight of an autogiro, a flying machine that operates on a different principle than a helicopter; its rotor is not powered but obtains lift by its mechanical rotation as the autogiro moves forward through the air. An autogiro has the advantage of a relatively short takeoff and a near vertical descent. The subsequent success of Cierva's autogiros and those of his competitors seemed to cast a pall on the future of helicopter development. Autogiros were rapidly improved and were manufactured in several countries, seeming to fill such a useful niche that they temporarily overshadowed the helicopter. Ironically, however, the technology of the rotor head and rotor blade developed for the autogiro contributed importantly to the development of the successful helicopter, which in time made the autogiro obsolete.

In 1936 Germany stepped to the forefront of helicopter development with the Focke Achgelis Fa 61, which had two three-bladed rotors mounted on outriggers and powered by a 160-horsepower radial engine. The Fa 61

AUTOGIROS

The autogiro (also spelled autogyro) was for many years in the early 20th century the most reasonable alternative to the helicopter as a means of vertical flight. The machine employed a propeller for forward motion and a freely rotating, unmotorized rotor for lift. Because the rotor is not powered, the autogiro does not have to contend with torque (the tendency of the aircraft to turn in the opposite direction of the rotor) and thus avoided many of the control problems that impeded the development of the helicopter. The autogiro's rotor is designed so that a blade set at a low positive angle of pitch will rotate automatically as long as an airstream is kept flowing through the rotor (autorotation). As the autogiro is propelled forward through the air, with a stream of air flowing upward through its rotor, lift is generated. Control is effected in part through a universal joint at the rotor head, which tilts the blades creating a force that pulls the autogiro in the direction of the tilt. An elevator and rudder are maintained within the propeller slipstream for additional control.

Autogiros brought aviators closer to the dream of landing vertically, but they still had to taxi for takeoff, and they required a forward airspeed in order to drive the rotor. By contrast, the helicopter, with its engine-driven rotor, was capable of both vertical takeoff and landing. Prospects for commercial development of the autogiro evaporated with the success of the more efficient helicopter after World War II.

had controllable cyclic pitch and set numerous records, including, in 1938, an altitude flight of 3,418 metres (11,243 feet) and a cross-country flight of 230 km (143 miles). In 1938 the German aviator Hanna Reitsch became the world's first female helicopter pilot by flying the Fa 61 inside the Deutschland-Halle in Berlin. It was both a technical and a propaganda triumph. Germany continued its helicopter development during World War II and was the first to place a helicopter, the Flettner Kolibri, into mass production.

In the United States, after many successes with commercial flying boats, Igor Sikorsky turned his attention to helicopters once again, and after a long period of development he made a successful series of test flights of his VS-300 in 1939–41. Essentially a test aircraft designed for easy and rapid modification, the VS-300 was small (weighing about 500 kg, or 1,100 pounds) and was powered by a 65-horsepower Lycoming engine. Yet it possessed the features that characterize most modern helicopters: a single main three-bladed rotor, with collective pitch, and a tail rotor. As successful as the VS-300 was, however, it also clearly showed the difficulties that all subsequent helicopters would experience in the development process. For many years, compared with conventional aircraft, helicopters were underpowered, difficult to control, and subject to much higher dynamic stresses that caused material and equipment failures. Yet the VS-300 led to a long line of Sikorsky helicopters, and it influenced their development in a number of countries, including France, England, Germany, and Japan.

After World War II the commercial use of helicopters developed rapidly in many roles, including fire fighting, police work, agricultural crop spraying, mosquito control, medical evacuation, and carrying mail and passengers.

The expanding market brought additional competitors into the field, each with different approaches to the problem of vertical flight. The Bell Aircraft Corporation, under the leadership of Arthur Young, began its long, distinguished history of vertical-flight aircraft with a series of prototypes that led to the Bell Model 47, one of the most significant helicopters of all time, incorporating an articulated, gyro-stabilized, two-blade rotor. Frank Piasecki created the Piasecki Helicopter Corporation; its designs featured a tandem-rotor concept. The use of twin tandem

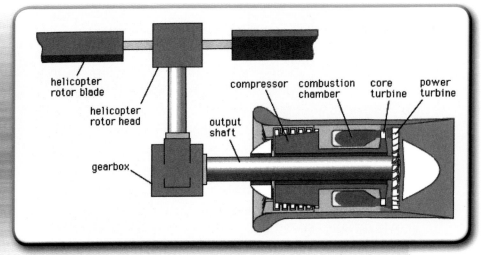

Turboshaft engine driving a helicopter rotor as propulsor. Copyright Encyclopædia Britannica, Inc.; rendering for this edition by Rosen Educational Services

rotors enabled helicopters to grow to almost twice their previous size without the difficulty of creating very large rotor blades. In addition, the placement of the twin rotors provided a large centre of gravity range. The competition was international, with rapid progress made in the Soviet Union, the United Kingdom, France, Italy, and elsewhere.

To an even greater extent than fixed-wing aircraft, the development of the helicopter had been limited by engine power. Reciprocating engines were heavy, noisy, and less efficient at high altitude. The first application of jet-engine technology to the helicopter was accomplished in 1951 by the Kaman Aircraft Corporation's HTK-1, which had Kaman's patented aerodynamic servo-controlled rotors in the "synchropter" configuration (i.e., side-by-side rotors with intermeshing paths of blade travel).

In conventional aircraft the power of the jet engine was used primarily for increased speed. In the helicopter the thrust of the jet turbine had to be captured by a gearbox that would turn the rotor. The jet engine had many advantages for the helicopter—it was smaller, weighed less than a piston engine of comparable power, had far less vibration, and used less expensive fuel. The French SNCA-S.E. 3130 Alouette II made its first flight on March 12, 1955, powered by a Turbomeca Artouste II turbine engine. It rapidly became one of the most influential helicopters in the world and started a trend toward jet-powered helicopters everywhere.

There are now a vast number of helicopter types available on the market, ranging from small two-person private helicopters through large passenger-carrying types to work vehicles capable of carrying huge loads to remote places. All of them respond to the basic principles of flight, but, because of the unique nature of the helicopter's rotor and control systems, the techniques for flying them differ. There are other types of vertical-lift aircraft, whose controls and techniques are often a blend of the conventional aircraft and the helicopter. They form a small part of the total picture of flight but are of growing importance.

PRINCIPLES OF FLIGHT AND OPERATION

Unlike fixed-wing aircraft, the helicopter's main airfoil is the rotating blade assembly (rotor) mounted atop its fuselage on a hinged shaft (mast) connected with the vehicle's engine and flight controls. In comparison to airplanes, the tail of a helicopter is somewhat elongated and the rudder smaller; the tail is fitted with a small antitorque rotor (tail rotor). The landing gear sometimes consists of a pair of skids rather than wheel assemblies.

The fact that the helicopter obtains its lifting power by means of a rotating airfoil (the rotor) greatly complicates the factors affecting its flight, for not only does the rotor turn but it also moves up and down in a flapping motion and is affected by the horizontal or vertical movement of the helicopter itself. Unlike the usual aircraft airfoils, helicopter rotor airfoils are usually symmetrical. The chord line of a rotor, like the chord line of a wing, is an imaginary line drawn from the leading edge to the trailing edge of the airfoil.

The relative wind is the direction of the wind in relation to the airfoil. In an airplane, the flight path of the wing is fixed in relation to its forward flight; in a helicopter, the flight path of the rotor advances forward (to the helicopter's nose) and then rearward (to the helicopter's tail) in the process of its circular movement. Relative wind is always considered to be in parallel and opposite direction to the flight path. In considering helicopter flight, the relative wind can be affected by the rotation of the blades, the horizontal movement of the helicopter, the flapping of the rotor blades, and wind speed and direction. In flight, the relative wind is a combination of the rotation of the rotor blade and the movement of the helicopter.

Like a propeller, the rotor has a pitch angle, which is the angle between the horizontal plane of rotation of the rotor disc and the chord line of the airfoil. The pilot uses the collective and cyclic pitch control (see below) to vary this pitch angle. In a fixed-wing aircraft, the angle of attack (the angle of the wing in relation to the relative wind) is important in determining lift. The same is true in a helicopter, where the angle of attack is the angle at which the relative wind meets the chord line of the rotor blade.

Angle of attack and pitch angle are two distinct conditions. Varying the pitch angle of a rotor blade changes its angle of attack and hence its lift. A higher pitch angle (up to the point of stall) will increase lift; a lower pitch angle will decrease it. Individual blades of a rotor have their pitch angles adjusted individually.

Rotor speed also controls lift—the higher the revolutions per minute (RPM), the higher the lift. However, the pilot will generally attempt to maintain a constant rotor RPM and will change the lift force by varying the angle of attack.

As with fixed-wing aircraft, air density (the result of air temperature, humidity, and pressure) affects helicopter performance. The higher the density, the more lift will be generated; the lower the density, the less lift will be generated. Just as in fixed-wing aircraft, a change in lift also results in a change in drag. When lift is increased by enlarging the angle of pitch and thus the angle of attack, drag will increase and slow down the rotor RPM. Additional power will then be required to sustain a desired RPM. Thus, while a helicopter is affected like a conventional aircraft by the forces of lift, thrust, weight, and drag, its mode of flight induces additional effects.

In a helicopter, the total lift and thrust forces generated by the rotor are exerted perpendicular to its plane of rotation. When a helicopter hovers in a windless condition, the plane of rotation of the rotor (the tip-path plane) is parallel to the ground, and the sum of the weight and drag forces are exactly balanced by the sum of the thrust and lift forces. In vertical flight, the components of weight and drag are combined in a single vector that is directed straight down; the components of lift and thrust are combined in a single vector that is directed straight up. To achieve forward flight in a helicopter, the plane of rotation of the rotor is tipped forward. (It should be understood that the helicopter's rotor mast does not tip but rather the individual rotor blades within the plane of rotation have their pitch angle varied.) For sideward flight, the plane of the rotation of the rotor is tilted in the direction desired. For rearward flight, the plane of the rotation of the rotor is tilted rearward.

Because the rotor is powered, there is an equal and opposite torque reaction, which tends to rotate the fuselage in a direction opposite to the rotor. This torque is offset by the tail rotor (antitorque rotor) located at the end of the fuselage. The pilot controls the thrust of the tail rotor by means of foot pedals, neutralizing torque as required.

There are other forces acting upon a helicopter not found in a conventional aircraft. These include the gyroscopic precession effect of the rotor—that is, the dissymmetry of lift created by the forward movement of the helicopter, resulting in the advancing blade having more lift and the retreating blade less. This occurs because the advancing blade has a combined speed of the blade velocity and the speed of the helicopter in forward flight, while the retreating blade has the difference between the blade velocity and the speed of the helicopter. This difference in speed causes a difference in lift—the advancing blade is moving faster and hence is generating more lift. If uncontrolled, this would result in the helicopter rolling. However, the difference in lift is compensated for by the blade flapping and by cyclic feathering (changing the angle of pitch). Because the blades are attached to a rotor hub by horizontal flapping hinges, which permit their movement in a vertical plane, the advancing blade flaps up, decreasing its angle of attack, while the retreating blade flaps down, increasing its angle of attack. This combination of effects equalizes the lift. (Blades also are attached to the hub by a vertical hinge, which permits each blade to move back and forth in the plane of rotation. The vertical hinge dampens out vibration and absorbs the effect of acceleration or deceleration.) In addition, in forward flight, the position of the cyclic pitch control causes a similar effect, contributing to the equalization of lift.

Other forces acting upon helicopters include coning, the upward bending effect on blades caused by centrifugal force; Coriolis effect, the acceleration or deceleration of the blades caused by the flapping movement bringing them closer to (acceleration) or farther away from (deceleration) the axis of rotation; and drift, the tendency of the tail rotor thrust to move the helicopter in hover.

CONTROL FUNCTIONS

A helicopter has four controls: collective pitch control, throttle control, antitorque control, and cyclic pitch control.

The collective pitch control is usually found at the pilot's left hand; it is a lever that moves up and down to change the pitch angle of the main rotor blades. Raising or lowering the pitch control increases or decreases the pitch angle on all blades by the same amount. An increase in the pitch angle will increase the angle of attack, causing both lift and drag to increase and causing the RPM of the rotor and the engine to decrease. The reverse happens with a decrease in pitch angle.

Because it is necessary to keep rotor RPM as constant as possible, the collective pitch control is linked to the throttle to automatically increase power when the pitch lever is raised and decrease it when the pitch lever is lowered. The collective pitch control thus acts as the primary control both for altitude and for power.

The throttle control is used in conjunction with the collective pitch control and is an integral part of its assembly. The throttle control is twisted outboard to increase rotor RPM and inboard to decrease RPM.

The antitorque controls are pedals linked to operate a pitch change mechanism in the tail rotor gearbox. A change in pedal position changes the pitch angle of the tail rotor to offset torque. As torque varies with every change of flight condition, the pilot is required to change pedal position accordingly. The antitorque control does not control the direction of flight.

It was stated above that the lift/thrust force is always perpendicular to the plane of rotation of the rotor. The cyclic pitch control, a stick-type control found to the pilot's right, controls the direction of flight by tipping the plane of rotation in the desired direction. The term *cyclic* derives from the sequential way each blade's pitch is changed so that it takes the flight path necessary to effect the change in direction.

THE HANG GLIDER

Hang gliders are aircraft of various configurations in which the pilot is suspended beneath the (usually fabric) wing to provide stability and control. They are normally launched from a high point. Hang gliders were developed by the pioneers of practical flight. In Germany, starting in 1891, Otto Lilienthal made several thousand flights before a fatal gliding accident in 1896. He published plans of his gliders and even supplied kits. In the United States collaboration between Augustus Herring and Octave Chanute resulted in successful flights of a biplane hang glider from dunes in Indiana at the southern end of Lake Michigan in 1896. In these early designs the pilot hung from the armpits on parallel bars beneath the wings, swinging hips and legs to control roll and shifting back and forth to influence pitch.

In the hands of an experienced pilot, hang gliders are capable of soaring (using rising air columns to obtain upward gliding movement). This capability has given rise to the sport of hang gliding. Modern hang gliding

OTTO LILIENTHAL

(b. May 23, 1848, Anklam, Prussia [now in Germany]–d. Aug. 10, 1896, Berlin)

Trained as a mechanical engineer, Otto Lilienthal established his own machine shop and flight factory following service in the Franco-Prussian War. He began to conduct studies of the forces operating on wings in a stream of air in the late 1870s. The results of that research appeared in 1889 in a book entitled *Der Vogelflug als Grundlage der Fliegekunst* ("Bird Flight as the Basis of Aviation") and in an important series of articles that provided a foundation for the final effort to achieve mechanical flight. As transmitted by Octave Chanute, Lilienthal's friend and American correspondent, the tables of data served as the starting point for the earliest aircraft designs of the Wright brothers.

Having explored the physical principles governing winged flight, Lilienthal began to design and build hang gliders on the basis of the information he had gathered. Between 1891 and 1896, he completed some 2,000 flights in at least 16 distinct glider types. His career as a builder and pilot of gliders coincided with the development of high-speed and stroboscopic photography. Images of Lilienthal flying through the air aboard his standard glider appeared around the globe in newspapers and the great illustrated magazines of the period. Those pictures convinced millions of readers in Europe and the United States that the age of flight was at hand. Lilienthal broke his back in a glider crash on Aug. 9, 1896, and died in a Berlin hospital the next day. Today he is seen as one of the most significant aeronautical pioneers in the years leading up to the Wright brothers.

emerged toward the end of the 1960s. In the early 1960s enthusiasts in California were gliding down coastal dunes on homebuilt delta-shaped wings they had adapted from kite designs developed by Francis Rogallo and his wife, Gertrude. The Rogallos' kites had attracted attention because of NASA's interest in using them for spacecraft retrieval. On the dunes cheap materials such as bamboo and plastic sheeting were used, and the parallel-bar control method remained. Around the same time, water-ski showmen in Australia were flying on flat kites towed behind speedboats. They were able to control these notoriously unstable flat kites by using swing seats that allowed their entire body weight to effect pitch and roll—a great improvement on the parallel-bar method. When a Rogallo wing was fitted with a swing seat by John Dickenson, in Sydney, Australia, the modern hang glider was born.

By the early 1970s the sport had spread throughout the United States and into Europe. Aircraft-quality materials began to be used, and glide performance increased steadily through improvements in wing and harness design. The original Rogallos with a seated pilot had glide ratios of about 3:1. That is, for every three feet traveled forward, they would descend one foot. By 1999 glide ratios had reached 15:1. In addition to the now-traditional delta-shaped flexible wings, a new generation of rigid, tailless hang gliders has become popular, in which carbon fibre and other composite materials provide the required blend of lightness and strength. Glide ratios in excess of 20:1 are possible, coupled with top speeds of about 100 km (60 miles) per hour, yet they can still launch and land at little more than walking pace.

Like all other engineless aircraft, hang gliders use gravity as the source of propulsion, so they are always sinking downward, just as a skier goes downhill. However, by seeking air that is moving upward faster than the aircraft is sinking, skilled pilots can remain aloft for hours. Typical sources for such lift occur where wind is deflected upward by a hill or mountain ridge or in columns of warm air called "thermals," which are caused by the sun heating the Earth's surface unevenly. Such is the efficiency of modern hang gliders that the world straight distance record, set in 2001, is 700.6 km (435.1 miles). Hang gliders are highly maneuverable, and their safety record compares well with that of other aviation sports.

Internationally, hang gliding is under the control of the Fédération Aéronautique Internationale (FAI). World championships have been held, usually in alternate years, ever since the first in Kössen, Austria, in 1975.

THE ULTRALIGHT

Ultralights were originally hang gliders adapted for power by the installation of small engines similar to those used in chain saws. However, they have matured into specially designed aircraft of very low weight and power but with flying qualities similar to conventional light aircraft. They are intended primarily for pleasure flying, although advanced models are now used for training, police patrol, and other

Whooping cranes following an ultralight aircraft. International Crane Foundation, Baraboo, WI

General Atomics MQ-1 Predator, a reconnaissance unmanned aerial vehicle of the U.S. Air Force, 2006. Dave Cibley—214th Reconnaissance Group/ U.S. Air Force

work, including a proposed use in combat. Experimental ultralights have been designed to make use of human and solar power. These are very lightweight, sophisticated aircraft, designed with heavy reliance on computers and using the most modern materials.

The first great exponent of ultralight aircraft was Paul MacCready (1925–2007), an American aerodynamicist who started sailplaning in 1947 and was U.S. soaring champion in 1948, 1949, and 1953, as well as international champion in 1956. He was head of his own firm, AeroVironment, in Pasadena, Calif., working on the improvement of air quality, the conservation of energy, and the derivation of power from wind and water. On Aug. 23, 1977, at Shafter Airport near Bakersfield, Calif., MacCready's *Gossamer Condor,* pedaled and piloted by 137-pound (62-kg) Bryan Allen, a bicyclist and hang-glider enthusiast, completed the course required to win the Kremer Prize of £50,000 ($95,000), clearing a 10-foot- (3-metre-) high start-and-finish line while making a figure-eight flight around two pylons set half a mile apart. The total distance flown was 1.15 miles (1.85 km) in 6 minutes 27.05 seconds, at a top speed of 11 miles (18 km) per hour. The 70-pound (32-kg) plane had a 96-foot (29-metre) wingspan.

A subsequent, more streamlined MacCready plane, the *Gossamer Albatross,* was pedaled and piloted by Allen from near Folkestone, Kent, Eng., to Cape Gris-Nez, France, a distance of 23 miles (37 km), in 2 hours 49 minutes, on June 12, 1979. This flight won the £100,000 Kremer Prize for the first man-propelled flight across the English Channel. The plane had a wingspan of 93 feet 10 inches (28.6 metres), weighed 70 pounds (32 kg), and was constructed of Mylar, polystyrene, and carbon-fibre rods.

On July 7, 1981, the *Solar Challenger,* a solar-powered plane designed by MacCready, flew from the Pointoise Cormeilles airport, near Paris, to the Manston Royal Air Force Base, in Kent, Eng., a distance of 160 miles (258 km), in 5 hours 23 minutes at an average speed of about 30 miles (48 km) per hour and a cruising altitude of 11,000 feet (3,350 metres). The pilot was Stephen Ptacek, weighing 122 pounds (55 kg). The plane, powered by 16,128 solar cells connected

Bertrand Piccard, 1999. Breitling SA

to two electric motors, weighed 210 pounds (95 kg) and had a wingspan of 47 feet (14.3 metres).

Macready's work has been continued by Bertrand Piccard (1958–), a Swiss aviator who in 1999, with British co-pilot Brian Jones, completed the first nonstop circum-navigation of the globe by balloon. In 2003, Piccard—with Swiss engineer and pilot André Borschberg—launched Solar Impulse, a project that had the ultimate goal of developing and launching a solar-powered airplane capable of circumnavigating the globe. A major step toward that goal was taken when a Solar Impulse plane piloted by Borschberg completed a 26-hour flight over Switzerland on July 7–8, 2010, becoming the first solar-powered aircraft to fly through the night.

CHAPTER 7

AIRPORTS

A n airport is a site and installation for the takeoff and landing of aircraft. An airport usually has paved runways and maintenance facilities and serves as a terminal for passengers and cargo.

The requirements for airports have increased in complexity and scale since the earliest days of flying. Before World War II the landing and takeoff distance of most passenger-transport aircraft was at most 600 metres (2,000 feet). Additional clear areas were provided for blind landings or bad-weather runs, but the total area involved rarely exceeded 200 hectares (500 acres).

It was not until the general introduction of heavy monoplanes for transport, such as the Douglas DC-3, during the late 1930s that extensive takeoff and landing distances were needed. Even then, the prewar airfields at New York City (La Guardia), London (Croydon), Paris (Le Bourget), and Berlin (Tempelhof) were laid out on sites close to the city centres. Because even transport aircraft of the period were relatively light, paved runways were a rarity. Croydon, Tempelhof, and Le Bourget, for example, all operated from grass strips only. Early airports were also major centres of leisure activity, often attracting more visitors than passengers. In 1939 La Guardia Airport attracted almost 250,000 visitors per month, reaching a peak of 7,000 in one day, compared with a maximum daily throughput of only 3,000 passengers. In 1929 Berlin's airport reported 750,000 visitors and boasted a restaurant that could seat 3,000 people on the roof of the passenger terminal. The status of prewar airports as major social centres was reflected in their design, especially where the requirements of catering, observation decks, and parking were paramount. Indeed, the requirements of aircraft and passengers were not at all dominant at early airfields.

Much long-distance air transport was handled by the large seaplanes known as flying boats or clippers. These aircraft, though slow and of limited range, offered a level of comfort that was necessary for long-distance travel. Air terminal facilities were necessarily constructed close to large open stretches of water. La Guardia Airport and Santos Dumont Airport in Rio de Janeiro are examples of airports that still operate on sites originally chosen for their ability to handle large seaplanes. The large facilities at Southampton Water in the United Kingdom have now disappeared, but the artificial lake at Linate Airport near Milan, Italy, is still to be found close to the present administration facilities.

The vast majority of airfields throughout the world are still relatively simple facilities. Even now, many have unpaved runways or at most lightly paved runways with tiny terminal or administration buildings, a rudimentary control tower, and crude landing aids. Such facilities can deal only with light aircraft and a negligible flow of passengers or freight. Heavy air traffic, on the other hand, is now almost entirely handled by sophisticated airport facilities that can accommodate the needs of crew, passengers, and freight and the great range of aircraft types that have evolved to meet the needs of modern air transport and general aviation.

More than 100 airports around the world now handle at least 10 million passengers each per year; nearly half of these are in the United States. Dozens of airports regularly move more than 30 million passengers on a yearly basis, and almost a dozen, ranging from the

Aerial view of Chicago's O'Hare International Airport, showing runways and terminals plowed free of snow. O'Hare is one of the busiest airports in the United States. © Comstock/Jupiterimages

Hartsfield Atlanta International Airport in the U.S. state of Georgia to London Heathrow Airport in the United Kingdom to Beijing Capital International Airport in China, each handle more than 50 million. The Memphis (Tennessee) International Airport, the home airport of the FedEx Corporation's cargo service, and the Hong Kong International Airport are the world's largest cargo shippers, each of which handled nearly four million tons in 2007.

In order to meet the increasing demand for air travel, large transport aircraft powered by multiple jet and turboprop engines have been built. Such aircraft require extensive ground facilities, runways, taxiways, fire-fighting and rescue services, passenger- and cargo-handling facilities, access to car parking and public transport, lighting, navigational and approach aids, and various support facilities such as catering, meteorology, and governmental inspection. In order to be attractively convenient, the complex of activities and facilities that make up a modern airport must be located sufficiently close to the main centres of world population. At the same time, they must be adequately distant, so that the environmental problems associated with the noise of large aircraft and the activities of large numbers of passengers, workers, and visitors do not become intolerable to the cities that are served.

MODERN AIRPORTS

The largest airports in the world employ more than 100,000 workers each. They are immensely complex entities with regard to the physical facilities that they comprise, the organizations that are active within their boundaries, and the services that are provided in conjunction with their operation.

Physical facilities include runways, taxiways, aprons, and strips, which are used for the landing and takeoff of aircraft, for the maneuvering and positioning of aircraft on the ground, and for the parking of aircraft in order to load and discharge passengers and cargo. For the safe landing and takeoff of aircraft, lighting and radio navigational aids are provided. These are supplemented by airfield markings, signs and signals, and air traffic control facilities. Support facilities on the airside of the field include meteorology, fire and rescue, power and other utilities, aircraft maintenance, and airport maintenance. Landside facilities are the passenger and cargo terminals and the access system, which includes parking, roads, public transport facilities, and loading and unloading areas.

Many organizations are involved in the operation of a modern airport. Overall management is usually in the control of an organization, authority, or company that holds a license to operate the facility. This license is granted subject to a judgment by the national civil aviation authorities that the managing body is fit and competent to run an airport within national and, if applicable, international laws governing safety and operations. While overall responsibility for efficient, safe, and legal operation lies with the airport management, many of the individual services at an airport are provided by other organizations. Such organizations include airlines; air traffic control authorities; ground handling companies; fixed-base operators; concessionaires; security organizations; governmental agencies responsible for customs, immigration, health control, and police; support companies providing flight catering, fueling, aircraft engineering, and maintenance; aero clubs; and flying schools. Since the early 1980s, when privatization began to sweep through civil aviation, terminal-operation companies have also become more frequent, such as those that own terminals in Birmingham, Eng.; Brussels; and Toronto.

Airport services related to the aircraft are frequently referred to as airside. Many of these services are concentrated on the apron, or ramp, which is that part of the operational surface adjacent to the terminals where aircraft are maneuvered or parked. They include the apron handling of aircraft, airside passenger transfer to the aircraft, the handling of baggage and cargo, aircraft fueling, catering and cabin cleaning, engine starting, deicing, ground power and air-conditioning, and minor maintenance engineering. Other airside services are runway inspection, lighting and navigational aids, fire fighting and rescue, airside maintenance, and air traffic control. Among the landside services are those related to ground passenger handling; these include check-in, security, customs and immigration, baggage delivery, information, catering, cleaning and maintenance, shops and concessionary facilities, automobile rental, ground transportation, porters, special help for the elderly and handicapped, automobile parking, and public transportation (including taxis). In addition, because airports employ such a large number of workers, extensive provision must be made for their daily requirements.

OPERATIONAL REQUIREMENTS

It is obvious even to the most casual observer that there is a large variation in the appearance and layout of airport facilities. Simple airports designed to accommodate light aircraft are essentially similar, but, as airports become larger and more complex, thus accommodating more passengers and cargo, their individual requirements affect their layouts and ensure that each becomes recognizably different.

The principal determinants of airport layout are the number of runways and their orientation, the shape of the available site, and constraints at the site both on the ground and in the air. The location and orientation of runways is governed in turn by the need to avoid obstacles, particularly during landing and takeoff procedures. For the largest airports, obstacles to air navigation must be considered up to about 15 km (10 miles) from the runways. Runway configurations must also ensure that, for 95 percent of the time, aircraft can approach and take off without either crosswinds or tailwinds that would inhibit operations. At the smallest airports, light aircraft are unable to operate in crosswinds greater than 10 knots; at all airports, operation in tailwinds in excess of 10 knots is not recommended by aircraft manufacturers (10 knots, or nautical miles per hour, is equal to about 12 statute miles per hour or 19 km per hour).

RUNWAY CONFIGURATIONS

The operational capacity of an airport, which is usually defined as the maximum possible number of aircraft landings and takeoffs, is determined by the number of runways that are available for use at any one time. The vast majority of airports around the world have the simplest possible layout, a single runway. Where crosswinds would be high for an unacceptable proportion of operational time, a two-runway configuration is necessary, usually in the form of a main runway and an auxiliary crosswind runway. Depending on the shape of the site and the availability of land, the crosswind facility can take on a crossed configuration or an open or closed V layout. Where visibility is good and aircraft can operate under visual flight rules (VFR), operational capacity increases from the lowest level, crossed runways, through the closed V and open V configurations. However, in poor visibility or under certain conditions of very heavy air traffic, aircraft must operate under the strict instructions and rules of air traffic control and instrument operation; these are called instrument

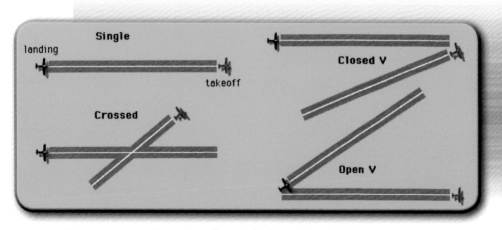

Four runway configurations. Copyright Encyclopædia Britannica, Inc.; rendering for this edition by Rosen Educational Services

flight rules (IFR). Under such conditions, crosswind runways cannot be used simultaneously with main runways, so that the capacities of the crossed and V configurations are equivalent to that of a single runway.

An increase in operational capacity under VFR is possible with the use of a close parallel runway configuration. Most very large airports must be assured of adequate capacity even under IFR conditions, and this can be achieved by separating the parallel runways by a minimum of 1,035 metres (3,400 feet), which was the distance approved by the International Civil Aviation Organization on Nov. 9, 1995. This independent parallel configuration permits simultaneous independent landings and takeoffs on both runways. Munich Airport exemplifies this type of configuration. Even greater capacity is possible using a four-runway configuration of independent close parallels,

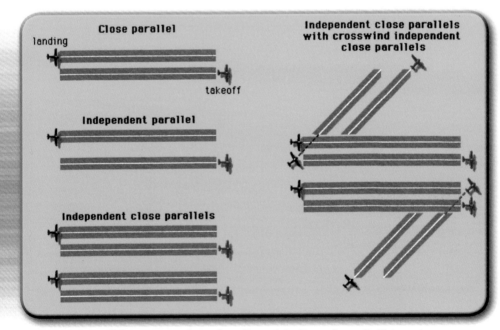

Four parallel runway configurations. Copyright Encyclopædia Britannica, Inc.; rendering for this edition by Rosen Educational Services

as is the case at Los Angeles International Airport. With such a configuration, even under IFR, it is possible for two aircraft to land simultaneously while two other aircraft take off. A number of the world's largest airports have master plans that feature eight runways in the form of independent close parallels supplemented by other close parallels that are capable of crosswind operation. However, with passenger aircraft increasing in size, most can now operate in crosswinds of 20 knots and above. This reduces the likelihood that configurations with four crosswind runways will ever be constructed.

RUNWAY PAVEMENTS

Until the introduction of heavy monoplane aircraft in the latter part of the 1930s, civil air-transport aircraft were able to operate from grass runways with takeoff distances of less than 600 metres (2,000 feet). The advent of heavy aircraft such as the DC-3 required the provision of paved runways; at the same time, takeoff distances increased to more than 900 metres (3,000 feet). The length requirements for runways continued to increase into the mid-1970s, when large civilian aircraft such as the Douglas DC-8 and some models of the Boeing 747 required almost 3,600 metres (12,000 feet) of runway at sea level. (Even longer runways were necessary at higher elevations or where high ambient air temperatures occurred during operations.) The trend toward increasing runway lengths caused many problems at existing civilian airports, where runways had to be extended in order to accommodate the new aircraft. Ultimately, pressure by airport operators and the development of turbofan jet engines arrested and finally reversed the trend. Since the 1970s, runway length requirements have actually decreased, and the takeoff and climb performance of civilian aircraft has improved substantially. This has brought a dual benefit in reducing the area of land required by an airport and also in reducing the area around the airport that is adversely affected by noise on takeoff.

At all but the smallest airports, pavements are now provided for runways, taxiways, aprons, and any other areas where aircraft are maneuvered. Pavements must be designed in such a way that they can bear the loads imposed by aircraft without failure. A pavement must be smooth and stable under conditions of loading during its expected or economic life. It should be free from dust and other particles that could be blown up and ingested into engines, and it must be capable of spreading and transmitting an aircraft's weight to the existing subsoil (or subgrade) in a manner that precludes subsoil failure. Another function of the pavement is to prevent weakening of the subsoil by moisture intrusion, especially from rainfall and frost.

Airfield pavements are of two types, rigid and flexible. Rigid pavements are constructed of portland cement concrete slabs resting on a prepared subbase of granular material or directly on a granular subgrade. Load is transmitted through the slabs to the underlying subgrade by flexure of the slabs. Flexible pavements are constructed of several thicknesses of asphalt or bituminous concrete layers overlying a base of granular material on a prepared subgrade. They spread the concentrated aircraft wheel loads throughout their depth until the load at the base of the pavement is less than the strength of the in situ soil. At all depths the strength of the pavement should be at least equal to the loads placed upon it by aircraft wheels. The choice of pavement type is often determined by economics. In some parts of the world, Portland cement concrete is cheaper than asphalt; in other parts, the converse is true. For certain parts of the airfield, however, asphaltic concrete is an unsuitable material for pavement construction because of its vulnerability to damage by aviation fuel. Therefore, even at airports where flexible airfield pavements are generally in use, it is usual for concrete pavements to be used where aircraft stand on the aprons and at runway ends where fuel spillage is frequent.

NAVIGATIONAL AIDS, LIGHTING, AND MARKING

Only the simplest airfields are designed for operations conducted under visual meteorological conditions (VMC). These facilities operate only in daylight, and the only guidance they are required to offer is a painted runway centreline and large painted numbers indicating the magnetic bearing of the runway. Larger commercial airports, on the other hand, must also operate in the hours of darkness and under instrument meteorological conditions (IMC), when horizontal visibility is 600 metres (2,000 feet) or less and the cloud base (or "decision height") is 60 metres (200 feet) or lower. In order to assist aircraft in approaches and takeoffs and in maneuvering on the ground, such airports are equipped with sophisticated radio navigational aids (navaids) and visual aids in the form of lighting and marking.

NAVIGATIONAL AIDS

The most common form of navaid used for the approach phase of aircraft descent is the instrument landing system (ILS). This is a radio signal that is beamed along the centreline of the runway and at the correct angle of approach (usually 3° above the horizontal). The beam is intercepted by an approaching aircraft up to 24 km (15 miles) from the threshold of the runway. Information is given concerning position above and below the glide slope and deviation to the right or left of centreline; consequently, the pilot is able to determine from cockpit instruments a deviation of the aircraft from the proper approach.

Additional approach information is given visually to the pilot in the form of lighting approach aids. Two systems of approach aids are in use: the visual approach slope indicator system (VASIS) and the more modern precision approach path indicator (PAPI). Both work on the principle of guiding lights that show white when the pilot is above the proper glide slope and red when below.

AIRFIELD LIGHTING

Visual guidance to approaching aircraft is also provided by approach lighting systems, a configuration of high-intensity white lights running along the centreline of the runway and extending up to 600 metres (2,000 feet) beyond the threshold. At airfields where aircraft operate in very poor visibility, touchdown-zone lighting is provided over the first 900 metres (3,000 feet) from the runway threshold. These lights, set in patterns flush with the runway pavement, provide guidance up to the final moment of touchdown.

The runway itself is strongly delineated by a variety of guidance light systems. The threshold is designated by a line of green lights, and the edges and centreline are delineated by white lights that shine toward the maneuvering aircraft at regular intervals. The pilot is warned of the approaching runway end by a line of red lights at the end of the usable pavement. Taxiways are delineated by blue edge lights and by green centreline lights that also appear at regular intervals.

RUNWAY MARKINGS

Considerable additional visual guidance is given to pilots by painted markings on the runway. The form of marking indicates at a glance whether radio instrument guidance is available at any particular airfield. On precision instrument runways, the runway edges are indicated by painted lines, and distances along the runway from the threshold are indicated by pavement markings. In addition, touchdown-zone markings are painted on the pavement immediately after the threshold, providing vital visual guidance during the moments immediately before touchdown when all lighting may be obscured by fog.

AIR TRAFFIC CONTROL

In the vicinity of airports—especially large airports, where in peak conditions as many as three landing or takeoff operations may occur every minute—the control of aircraft in the air is a difficult but extremely important operation. Aircraft require very large amounts of airspace,

Interior view of an airport traffic control tower at dusk. The airport traffic control tower manages takeoffs and all movement within the airport's terminal control area. © Comstock/Jupiterimages

but at the same time the risk of collision must be set at very low, almost negligible, levels. Because aircraft are concentrated in the airspace around airports, acceptable levels of collision risk can be achieved only by strict adherence to procedures that are set out and monitored by air traffic control authorities.

An aircraft in flight follows en route air traffic control instructions as it flies through successive flight information regions (FIRs). Upon approaching an airport at which a landing is to be made, the aircraft passes into the terminal control area (TCA). Within this area, there may be a greatly increased density of air traffic, and this is closely monitored on radar by TCA controllers, who continually instruct pilots on how to navigate within the area. The aircraft is then brought into the final approach pattern, at which point control passes to the approach controller, who monitors the aircraft to the runway itself. Once on the runway, the pilot is given instructions on ground maneuvers by the ground controller, whose responsibility is to avoid conflicting movements of aircraft in the operational area of the airfield. The ground controller gives the pilot instructions on reaching the apron stand position via the appropriate turnoffs and taxiways. Final positioning may be the responsibility of an apron controller. Departing aircraft go through a reverse procedure, whereby control is passed from ground control to departure control to terminal control area and, finally, to en route control.

CARGO FACILITIES

Less than 1 percent of all freight tonnage is carried by air. Nonetheless, this statistic significantly underestimates the importance of air freight because, in value of cargo moved, air transport dominates all other modes. For example, although Heathrow Airport handles only about a million tons of freight per year, in value of throughput it ranks as Britain's premier port.

As is the case with passenger facilities, freight terminals vary greatly in the volumes of material handled. Consequently, the scale of the building facilities and the nature of the handling methods also vary. Because only 10 percent of air cargo is carried loose or in bulk, all modern air-cargo facilities are designed to handle containers. In countries where labour is cheap and where freight throughputs at the terminal are not high, freight-handling systems can still be economically designed around the manhandling concept. This is not feasible in developed countries, where labour costs are high. Even at facilities with small throughputs, freight is moved by mobile mechanical equipment such as stackers, tugs, and forklift trucks. At high-volume facilities, a mixture of mobile equipment and complex fixed stacking and movement systems must be used. The fixed systems, which require complex engineering design and maintenance, are known as transfer vehicles (TVs) and elevating transfer vehicles (ETVs).

In the design of air-cargo facilities, special attention must be given to the handling of very heavy and oversized freight, perishables, urgent materials such as serums and human donor organs, high-value goods such as diamonds and gold, hazardous goods, and livestock.

An area of very fast growth in the air-cargo business is specialized movement by integrated carriers such as the U.S.-based FedEx Corporation, which offers door-to-door delivery of small packages at premium rates. In its early years, this type of freight grew by more than 17 percent per annum. Cargo terminals for the small-package business are designed and constructed separately from conventional air-cargo terminals. They operate in a different manner, with all packages being cleared on an overnight basis.

ENVIRONMENTAL IMPACT

Large airports are actually urban complexes in which high-population activity centres are closely associated with very extensive paved areas. Typically a large airport can, on a daily basis, handle more than 100,000 passengers and support a working population of more than 50,000 employees. The sewage system of such an airport must cope with large daily flows of sanitary sewage effluent and, in addition, must accommodate runoff from rain and snow accumulating over several hundred acres of impervious pavement. The scale of the sewage problem at many large airports is such that some facilities have their own sewage treatment plants, especially for sanitary sewage. Because many airports are situated on low-lying ground, which is more likely to provide the flat land necessary for airstrips, the sewage system must often include extensive pumping facilities.

Growing concern about the environment combined with the increasing scale of activity at many airports has meant that runoff water can no longer be drained directly into bodies of surface water such as rivers and lakes. In particular, deicing chemicals used on aircraft and airfield pavements and cleaning chemicals used in aircraft maintenance are serious contaminants of groundwater and surface water. Consequently, some airports are required to provide at least primary treatment of all runoff discharges, and there are legal restrictions on the nature of the chemicals that can be used. In order to prevent groundwater pollution, Munich Airport was designed to accommodate existing flows of surface water across the entire site and was also provided with extensive arrangements for the recycling of deicing chemicals.

By the early 1960s, aircraft noise in the vicinity of urban airports had become a major problem. The cause of the problem was a rapidly increasing number of aircraft movements and the introduction of the first generation of turbojet aircraft with low climb performance, such as the early models of the Boeing 707 and the Douglas DC-8. Subsequently, public objections arose to the planned expansion of most urban airports. These objections often held up expansion for many years and, in cities such as London and Munich, ultimately severely modified the development of new airports. In addition, noise curfews were introduced at many existing airports, such as John F. Kennedy in New York, London's Heathrow, and Kingsford Smith Airport near Sydney.

In response to national and international regulations aimed at certifying only quieter aircraft, major efforts have been made by aircraft manufacturers to reduce noise at the source. Successive generations of aircraft have been banned as they failed to meet increasingly severe requirements introduced by the International Civil Aviation Organization and the U.S. Federal Aviation Administration. The introduction of high-bypass turbofan engines and aircraft with high climb performance have helped considerably in reducing noise.

Airports can diminish aircraft noise in a number of ways. Hours of operation can be limited through the use of night curfews, night noise having been found much more objectionable to the public than day noise. Noisy aircraft can be restricted or even banned. Runways can be selected to limit or spread noise more evenly over the community, and approach and departure routes can be designated over less-populated areas. Airlines can also be encouraged to modify approach and departure gradients and operating procedures in order to reduce engine thrust over highly populated areas. The performance of the operators is monitored, and offending operators have financial penalties imposed upon them. Using such methods, many major airports—even those that anticipate long-term growth in passenger numbers and aircraft movements—can significantly reduce the exposure of urban populations to aircraft noise.

AIRPORT SECURITY

Until the 1960s, airport security was relatively simple, requiring nothing more than civilian police to provide protection against conventional crimes such as theft, pickpocketing, vandalism, and breaking and entering. However, in the 1960s civil aviation became a recognized target for politically motivated crimes. These crimes came to include general acts of terrorism, such as mass shootings and bombings and, especially, aircraft hijacking.

Although the first aircraft hijacking occurred in 1931 in Peru, such events were rare, with no more than a handful each year, and generally without any political motive. However, by the late 1960s, politically motivated hijackings to Cuba had become common. In 1969, for example, there were 87 hijackings worldwide, of which 71 were related to Cuba, which typically granted political asylum to the hijackers.

The International Civil Aviation Organization (ICAO), which quickly recognized that passenger airliners had become political targets, responded in the decades of the 1960s and '70s with three major conventions covering "unlawful acts against civil aviation." To combat the crimes of hijacking and terrorism, the following international conventions established minimum conditions for appropriate security countermeasures to be adopted in an international context:

- Convention on Offences and Certain Other Acts Committed on Board Aircraft, commonly called the Tokyo Convention, was signed on Sept. 14, 1963, and went into force on Dec. 4, 1969—concerned with crimes on board aircraft, particularly any crime that jeopardizes the safety of the aircraft and its passengers;
- Convention for the Suppression of Unlawful Seizure of Aircraft, commonly called The Hague Convention, was signed on Dec. 16, 1970, and went into force on Oct. 14, 1971—concerned specifically with the offence of hijacking, with a recommendation that it should be made an extraditable offence for all member countries;
- Convention for the Suppression of Unlawful Acts Against the Safety of Civil Aviation, commonly called the Montreal Convention, was signed on Sept. 23, 1971, and went into force on Jan. 26, 1973—broadened the scope of The Hague Convention to include the crime of sabotage.

These conventions resulted in many ICAO recommendations for the enforcement of greater security at airports. However, because the ICAO has no national jurisdiction, the organization's recommendations needed to be translated into individual national laws. Following the Tokyo Convention, the ICAO measures were widely adopted by most national civil aviation authorities, although the efficiency of the security procedures adopted varied greatly throughout the world. Countries that had no history of domestic civil terrorism became overconfident in their security measures, believing that only international flights were real targets for terrorist attacks. However, as terrorist acts continued to occur against passenger airliners, security measures gradually became less lax in most jurisdictions.

Initially, the principal objective of security measures was to ensure that passengers could not board aircraft with weapons or explosives. Passengers were scanned with magnetometers and suspicious individuals selected for body searches; carry-on baggage was routinely passed through X-ray machines. Public access to the aprons and operational areas was denied, except for authorized staff, as was unnecessary access to the nonpublic areas of the terminal. As control of passengers and carry-on baggage tightened, hijackings were increasingly replaced by acts of sabotage to aircraft, carried out by explosive devices secreted in baggage carried in the airplane's hold. By the late 1990s, the ICAO had produced recommendations that all hold baggage should be screened for explosive and dangerous devices. The operational areas of civil airfields were enclosed by security fences, with manned access gates and visual surveillance of much of the areas by closed-circuit television.

In 2001, the September 11 attacks produced a sea change in much of the thinking surrounding airport security. In a period of two hours, a single terrorist organization wreaked an unprecedented level of destruction in the United States by using hijacked airliners as missiles. For the first time, civil transport aircraft, loaded with passengers and, most significantly, with a nearly full load of fuel, had been converted to destructive weapons.

Authorities responded to these hijackings with an intensification of security procedures at airports around the world. Passenger and baggage search procedures were made significantly more thorough, involving more careful screening for known terrorists (including the creation of various no-fly and watch lists of risky individuals) and potentially problematic carry-on items. Passenger terminals increased the level and sophistication of security equipment, the number of staff employed in security procedures, and the space provided for security operations. As a result, recommended check-in times for departing international passengers at many airports became as much as three hours before scheduled departure.

Hand baggage and checked baggage both became subject to strict scrutiny following Sept. 11, 2001. Many additional airports installed X-ray equipment, for spotting metal items in baggage or concealed in clothing, and massive electronic detection systems (EDS), which can detect trace molecules released by explosive materials. The massive weight of EDS equipment frequently requires structural modifications to existing buildings, and the size of the equipment often requires a reallocation of floor space. In many airports, installed security equipment now must be approved and certified by the national government.

Another problem for security at airports is the possibility of a car or truck being loaded with explosives and detonated near people or facilities. In particular, the threat from such "car bombs" forced greater caution with the location and operation of passenger pick-up areas and airport parking facilities. Parking garages that were integrated into the design of the passenger terminal pose a special danger. At those airports where parking design results in a threat to the safety of the terminal building from potential car bombs, operational procedures have been reevaluated and changed. In many cases, parking facilities integrated into the terminal itself have been closed.

The threat of terrorist attacks has meant that, for the foreseeable future and probably permanently, civil aviation cannot return to a situation of relaxed security. Eventually, access to airport terminals might require that all persons pass through some form of security check prior to check-in, that all passengers and baggage be thoroughly scrutinized for weapons and explosives, and that passengers undergo profiling interviews to identify potential problem travelers.

CONCLUSION

The dream of flight has progressed far beyond the days when people would watch the patterns of smoke rising into the air or the soaring of birds on the wind and wonder if it would be possible to emulate their action. Balloons, though surpassed as a means of air transport by fixed-wing airplanes, continue to be used for sport, pleasure, and scientific research, owing to the simplicity and reliability of the basic lighter-than-air concept.

Heavier-than-air craft—both fixed-wing airplanes and rotary-wing helicopters—have passed into the age of gas-turbine propulsion, advanced avionics, and lightweight composite materials. Their primacy as global transport is uncontested, though it is a primacy that is not without challenges in an era of rising fuel prices, growing concerns over air pollution, and wasteful land use. Perhaps most important in the minds of travelers is a greater need for security against mishaps and violence. Despite these challenges, the dream of flight, since its realization in the early 20th century, continues to inspire people's seemingly innate desire to defy space, time, and the force of gravity by transporting themselves through the air to far-off places.

❧APPENDIX

NOTABLE BALLOON FLIGHTS		
DATE	BALLOONISTS	DESCRIPTION
Aug. 8, 1709	Bartholomeu Lourenço de Gusmão (Brazil)	first model balloon flight
June 5, 1783	Joseph-Michel Montgolfier and Jacques-Étienne Montgolfier (France)	first demonstration flight of hot-air balloon
Aug. 27, 1783	Jacques-Alexandre-César Charles (France)	first demonstration flight of gas balloon
Nov. 21, 1783	Jean Pilâtre de Rozier and François Laurent (France)	first manned flight (hot-air)
Dec. 1, 1783	Jacques-Alexandre-César Charles and Marie-Noël Robert (France)	first manned flight in gas balloon
Dec. 1, 1783	Jacques-Alexandre-César Charles	first solo flight
June 23, 1784	Jean Pilâtre de Rozier and L.J. Proust (France)	first flight to exceed 50 km (31 miles)
Sept. 19, 1784	Marie-Noël Robert and Anne-Jean Robert (France)	first flight to exceed 100 km; 186 km (116 miles)
Jan. 7, 1785	Jean-Pierre Blanchard (France) and John Jeffries (U.S.)	first flight across the English Channel
June 15, 1785	Jean Pilâtre de Rozier and Pierre-Jules Romain (France)	first balloonist fatalities

Date	Balloonists	Description
Aug. 26, 1785	Jean-Pierre Blanchard and Chevalier de Lepinard (France)	first flight to exceed 200 km (124 miles)
June 2, 1794	Jean-Marie-Joseph Coutelle (France)	first use of a balloon (tethered) for military observations
Oct. 22, 1797	André-Jacques Garnerin (France)	first parachute descent from a balloon
Oct. 4, 1803	André-Jacques Garnerin and M. Aubert (France)	first flight to exceed 300 km (186 miles)
April 8, 1835	Richard Clayton (U.S.)	first flight to exceed 500 km (311 miles)
Nov. 7, 1836	Charles Green (U.K.)	flight from London to Germany; about 800 km (500 miles)
Sept. 2, 1849	François Arban (France)	first flight over the Alps
July 1, 1859	John Wise and John LaMountain (U.S.)	flight from St. Louis to Henderson, N.Y.; about 1,300 km (800 miles)
Sept. 23, 1870	Claude-Jules Durouf (France)	first balloon to carry mail out during the Siege of Paris
Oct. 29, 1912	Alfred Leblanc (France)	first flight to exceed 2,000 km (1,243 miles)
Feb. 10, 1914	Hans Rudolf Berliner, Alexander Haase, and A. Nicolai (Ger.)	first flight to exceed 3,000 km (1,864 miles)
April 13, 1963	Edward Yost and Donald Piccard (U.S.)	first flight over English Channel in hot-air balloon
Aug. 12–17, 1978	Ben L. Abruzzo, Maxie Leroy Anderson, and Larry M. Newman (U.S.)	first transatlantic flight; 5,001 km (3,107 miles)

DATE	BALLOONISTS	DESCRIPTION
Nov. 10–12, 1981	Ben L. Abruzzo, Larry M. Newman, Rocky Aoki, and Ron Clark (U.S.)	first transpacific flight; 8,383 km (5,209 miles)
Sept. 15–18, 1984	Joseph W. Kittinger (U.S.)	first solo transatlantic flight
July 2–3, 1987	Per Axel Lindstrand (Swed.) and Richard Branson (U.K.)	first transatlantic flight in hot-air balloon
Jan.16–17, 1991	Per Axel Lindstrand and Richard Branson	first transpacific flight in hot-air balloon
Feb. 17–21, 1995	Steve Fossett (U.S.)	first solo transpacific flight
March 3–21, 1999	Bertrand Piccard (Switz.) and Brian Jones (U.K.)	first around-the-world flight
June 19–July 3, 2002	Steve Fossett	first solo around-the-world flight

NOTABLE BALLOON ALTITUDE RECORDS

DATE	BALLOONISTS	ALTITUDE
April 24, 1804	Joseph-Louis Gay-Lussac and Jean-Baptiste Biot (France)	3,977 metres (2.5 miles)
Sept. 19, 1804	Joseph-Louis Gay-Lussac	7,016 metres (4.4 miles)
Sept. 5, 1862	James Glashier and Henry Tracey Coxwell (U.K.)	9,144 metres (5.7 miles)
July 31, 1901	Arthur Joseph Berson and R.J. Süring (Ger.)	10,800 metres (6.7 miles)
May 27, 1931	Auguste Piccard and Paul Kipfer (Switz.)	15,781 metres (9.8 miles)

DATE	BALLOONISTS	ALTITUDE
Oct. 23, 1934	Jean Piccard and Jeannette Piccard (U.S.)	17,550 metres (10.9 miles)
Nov. 11, 1935	Orvil A. Anderson and Albert W. Stevens (U.S.)	22,066 metres (13.7 miles)
June 2, 1957	Joseph W. Kittinger (U.S.)	29,300 metres (18.2 miles)
Oct. 8, 1958	Clifton M. McClure (U.S.)	30,175 metres (18.7 miles)
Aug. 16, 1960	Joseph W. Kittinger	31,333 metres (19.5 miles); highest successful parachute jump
May 4, 1961	Malcolm D. Ross and Victor A. Prather (U.S.)	34,668 metres (21.5 miles)
Oct. 27, 1972	U.S.	51,816 metres (32.2 miles); unmanned flight
June 6, 1988	Per Axel Lindstrand (Swed.)	19,811 metres (12.3 miles); hot-air balloon
Nov. 26, 2005	Vijaypat Singhania (India)	21,027 metres (13.1 miles); hot-air balloon

PIONEER AIRCRAFT

AIRPLANE	MAIDEN FLIGHT	WINGSPAN	LENGTH	WEIGHT
Ader Éole	1890	14 metres (45 feet 10 inches)	6.5 metres (21 feet 4 inches)	296 kg (653 pounds)

AIRPLANE	MAIDEN FLIGHT	WINGSPAN	LENGTH	WEIGHT
Lilienthal standard glider	1894	7.9 metres (26 feet)	4.19 metres (13 feet 1 inch)	
Chanute biplane glider	1896	4.9 metres (16 feet)	1.2 metres (4 feet)	14 kg (31 pounds)
Langley aerodrome No. 5	1896	4.3 metres (14 feet)	4.3 metres (14 feet)	11.8 kg (26 pounds)
Pilcher Hawk	1896	7.1 metres (23 feet 4 inches)	5.6 metres (18 feet 6 inches)	23 kg (50 pounds)
Ader Avion III	1897	17 metres (56 feet)		400 kg (882 pounds)
Wright flyer	1903	12.3 metres (40 feet 4 inches)	6.4 metres (21 feet 1 inch)	274 kg (605 pounds)
Santos-Dumont No. 14-*bis*	1906	12 metres (39 feet 4 inches)	10 metres (33 feet)	160 kg (350 pounds)
Voisin-Farman I	1907	10.2 metres (33 feet 6 inches)		520 kg (1,150 pounds)
June Bug	1908	12.9 metres (42 feet 6 inches)	8.4 metres (27 feet 6 inches)	
R.E.P. No. 2-*bis*	1908	9.6 metres (31 feet 6 inches)	8 metres (26 feet)	420 kg (925 pounds)
Bleriot XI	1909	8.52 metres (28 feet 6 inches)	7.63 metres (25 feet 6 inches)	326 kg (720 pounds)

Airplane	Maiden Flight	Wingspan	Length	Weight
Farman III	1909	10 metres (33 feet)	12 metres (39 feet 4 inches)	550 kg (1,213 pounds)
Curtiss Model E flying boat	1912	12.2 metres (40 feet)	7.9 metres (26 feet)	677 kg (1,490 pounds)

WORLD'S BUSIEST AIRPORTS BY TOTAL PASSENGER TRAFFIC (ENPLANING AND DEPLANING)

Rank	Airport	Serves	Airport Code	Total Passengers/ Yr
1	Hartsfield-Jackson Atlanta International Airport	Atlanta, Ga., U.S.	ATL	87,993,451
2	London Heathrow Airport	London, U.K.	LHR	66,037,578
3	Beijing Capital International Airport	Beijing, China	PEK	65,329,851
4	O'Hare International Airport	Chicago, Ill., U.S.	ORD	64,397,891
5	Tokyo International Airport	Tokyo, Japan	HND	61,903,656

Rank	Airport	Serves	Airport Code	Total Passengers/ Yr
6	Paris–Charles de Gaulle International Airport	Paris, France	CDG	57,884,954
7	Los Angeles International Airport	Los Angeles, Calif., U.S.	LAX	56,518,605
8	Dallas/ Fort Worth International Airport	Dallas/ Fort Worth, Texas, U.S.	DFW	56,030,457
9	Frankfurt Airport	Frankfurt, Germany	FRA	50,932,840
10	Denver International Airport	Denver, Colo., U.S.	DEN	50,167,485
11	Madrid-Barajas Airport	Madrid, Spain	MAD	48,248,890
12	John F. Kennedy International Airport	New York, N.Y., U.S.	JFK	45,912,430
13	Hong Kong International Airport	Hong Kong, China	HKG	45,560,888
14	Amsterdam Airport Schiphol	Amsterdam, Netherlands	AMS	43,569,553
15	Dubai International Airport	Dubai, United Arab Emirates	DXB	40,901,752

Rank	Airport	Serves	Airport Code	Total Passengers/ Yr
16	Bangkok International Suvarnabhumi Airport	Bangkok, Thailand	BKK	40,500,269
17	McCarran International Airport	Las Vegas, Nev., U.S.	LAS	40,460,310
18	George Bush Intercontinental Airport	Houston, Texas, U.S.	IAH	39,993,236
19	Phoenix Sky Harbor International Airport	Phoenix, Ariz., U.S.	PHX	37,824,982
20	San Francisco International Airport	San Francisco, Calif., U.S.	SFO	37,366,287
21	Singapore Changi Airport	Changi, Singapore	SIN	37,203,978
22	Guangzhou Baiyun International Airport	Guangzhou, China	CAN	37,048,550
23	Jakarta Soekarno-Hatta International Airport	Jakarta, Indonesia	CGK	36,466,823
24	Charlotte Douglas International Airport	Charlotte, N.C., U.S.	CLT	34,577,808

Rank	Airport	Serves	Airport Code	Total Passengers/ Yr
25	Miami International Airport	Miami, Fla., U.S.	MIA	33,886,025
Source: Airports Council International, "Preliminary World Airport Traffic 2009."				

WORLD'S BUSIEST AIRPORTS BY TOTAL MOVEMENTS (TAKEOFFS AND LANDINGS)

Rank	Airport	Serves	Airport Code	Total Movements/Yr
1	Hartsfield-Jackson Atlanta International Airport	Atlanta, Ga., U.S.	ATL	970,235
2	O'Hare International Airport	Chicago, Ill., U.S.	ORD	827,679
3	Dallas/ Fort Worth International Airport	Dallas/Fort Worth, Texas, U.S.	DFW	638,782
4	Denver International Airport	Denver, Colo., U.S.	DEN	606,006
5	George Bush Intercontinental Airport	Houston, Texas, U.S.	IAH	578,150
6	Los Angeles International Airport	Los Angeles, Calif., U.S.	LAX	545,210

RANK	AIRPORT	SERVES	AIRPORT CODE	TOTAL MOVEMENTS/YR
7	Paris–Charles de Gaulle International Airport	Paris, France	CDG	525,314
8	McCarran International Airport	Las Vegas, Nev., U.S.	LAS	511,064
9	Charlotte Douglas International Airport	Charlotte, N.C., U.S.	CLT	509,358
10	Beijing Capital International Airport	Beijing, China	PEK	488,495
11	Philadelphia International Airport	Philadelphia, Pa., U.S.	PHL	472,668
12	London Heathrow Airport	London, U.K.	LHR	466,393
13	Frankfurt Airport	Frankfurt, Germany	FRA	463,111
14	Phoenix Sky Harbor International Airport	Phoenix, Ariz., U.S.	PHX	457,207
15	Madrid–Barajas International Airport	Madrid, Spain	MAD	435,179
16	Minneapolis–St. Paul International Airport	Minneapolis–St. Paul, Minn., U.S.	MSP	432,604

RANK	AIRPORT	SERVES	AIRPORT CODE	TOTAL MOVEMENTS/YR
17	Detroit Metropolitan Wayne County Airport	Detroit, Mich., U.S.	DTW	432,589
18	John F. Kennedy International Airport	New York, N.Y., U.S.	JFK	412,980
19	Newark Liberty International Airport	Newark, N.J., U.S.	EWR	411,185
20	Toronto Pearson International Airport	Toronto, Ont., Canada	YYZ	407,736
21	Amsterdam Airport Schiphol	Amsterdam, Netherlands	AMS	406,969
22	Phoenix Deer Valley Airport	Phoenix, Ariz., U.S.	DVT	402,335
23	Munich Airport	Munich, Germany	MUC	396,805
24	San Francisco International Airport	San Francisco, Calif., U.S.	SFO	379,751
25	Salt Lake City International Airport	Salt Lake City, Utah, U.S.	SLC	372,354
Source: Airports Council International, "Preliminary World Airport Traffic 2009."				

GLOSSARY

actuate To put into mechanical action or motion.

adiabatic Occurring without loss or gain of heat.

aeolipile A steam turbine that consisted of a sphere with one or more projecting bent tubes, out of which steam passed and turned the sphere.

aeronaut One who pilots or travels in an airship or balloon.

ballast A heavy substance placed in such a way as to improve stability and control of a moving vehicle or vessel.

buoyancy The ability of a body to rise in fluid, gas, or air.

calorimeter An apparatus for measuring quantities of absorbed or emitted heat, or for determining specific heats.

cambered Curving or arching upward in the middle.

canard A small airfoil or projection located in front of an aircraft's wing that can increase the aircraft's performance.

coning The upward bending of the rotor blades of a helicopter as it lifts.

Coriolis effect An effect that causes material moving on a rotating planet to appear to be deflected to either the right or the left.

dirigible A lighter-than-air craft equipped with steering controls, also called simply an "airship."

fuselage The central body portion of an aircraft designed to accommodate crew and passengers or cargo.

gimbal A device that permits a body to incline freely in any direction or suspends it so that it will remain level when its support is tipped.

gondola An often spherical, airtight enclosure suspended from a balloon for carrying passengers or instruments.

hermetic Sealed in an airtight fashion.

lift An aerodynamic force perpendicular to the relative wind, resulting in an upward force that opposes the pull of gravity; necessary for flight.

monocoque A type of fuselage construction in which the outer skin carries all or a major part of the stresses.

ornithopter An aircraft designed to derive its chief support and propulsion from flapping wings.

pneumatic Moved or worked by air pressure.

propulsion The act or process of driving forward or onward by or as if by means of a force that imparts motion.

stratosphere Layer of the atmosphere above the troposphere.

tensile strength The greatest longitudinal stress a substance can bear without tearing apart.

trimotor An airplane powered by three engines.

troposphere The lowest region of Earth's atmosphere, where nearly all water vapour exists and essentially all weather occurs.

zeppelin A rigid airship consisting of a cylindrical trussed and covered frame supported by internal gas cells.

BALLOON FLIGHT

Tom D. Crouch, *Lighter Than Air: An Illustrated History of Balloons and Airships* (2009), covers the development of lighter-than-air flight from Archimedes to modern sport ballooning. Harold G. Dick and Douglas H. Robinson, *Golden Age of the Great Passenger Airships* (1985), focuses on the *Graf Zeppelin* and the *Hindenburg*. *Balloon Flying Handbook*, rev. ed. (2008), by the U.S. Federal Aviation Administration, is for student pilots learning to fly balloons as well as for experienced pilots seeking advanced proficiency.

AIRPLANES

Tom D. Crouch, *A Dream of Wings: Americans and the Airplane, 1875–1905* (1981, reissued 2002), is a study of the rise of a community of American engineers and scientists who laid the foundation for the invention of the airplane. Charles Harvard Gibbs-Smith, *The Rebirth of European Aviation, 1902–1908* (1974), describes the impact of the Wright brothers on European flight experimenters. Richard P. Hallion, *Taking Flight: Inventing the Aerial Age from Antiquity to the First World War* (2003), provides a good survey of the early history of flight. Robert Wohl, *A Passion for Wings: Aviation and the Western Imagination, 1908–1918* (1994, reissued 1996), is a beautifully illustrated study of the social and cultural impact of early flight.

R.E.G. Davies, *The World's Airlines* (1964; also published as *A History of the World's Airlines*, 1964, reprinted 1983), is an indispensable encyclopaedic reference. Roger E. Bilstein, *Flight in America: From the Wrights to the Astronauts*, 3rd ed. (2001), includes social and cultural commentary on airline trends as well as developments in general aviation. Oliver E. Allen et al., *The Airline Builders* (1981), is a superbly illustrated book and a colourful narrative about international activities during the 1920s and '30s. Terry Gwynn-Jones, *Farther and Faster: Aviation's Adventuring Years, 1909–1939* (1991), is an engrossing chronicle of record flights and personalities.

Walter J. Boyne and Donald S. Lopez (eds.), *The Jet Age: Forty Years of Jet Aviation* (1979), contains excellent articles by the principal engineers of the time. Bill Gunston, *World Encyclopedia of Aero Engines*, 5th ed. (2006), is an indispensable reference that charts the progress of all the main engine companies. Walter J. Boyne, *Clash of Wings* (1994), is a comprehensive overview of World War II aerial operations that includes the introduction of jet aircraft. John D. Anderson, Jr., *A History of Aerodynamics and Its Impact on Flying Machines* (1997), is a comprehensive, if demanding, history of aerodynamics. Bill Gunston, *Avionics* (1990), contains an in-depth history of the developments of modern avionics. Donald M. Patillo, *Pushing the Envelope* (1998), is an excellent review of the American aircraft industry, with insightful statistics.

HELICOPTERS

Basic Helicopter Handbook, rev. ed. (1978), prepared by the U.S. Federal Aviation Administration, is a well-illustrated primer on the principles of helicopter flight and structure. Walter J. Boyne and Donald S. Lopez (eds.), *Vertical Flight: The Age of the Helicopter* (1984), surveys the history and technology of helicopters and other aircraft designed for vertical flight. Mike Rogers, *VTOL Military Research*

Aircraft (1989), describes basic types of research and production vertical-takeoff aircraft.

AIRPORTS

Norman Ashford and Paul H. Wright, *Airport Engineering*, 3rd ed. (1992), comprehensively sets forth the planning, layout, and design of passenger and freight airports, including heliports and short takeoff and landing (STOL) facilities. Robert Horonjeff and Francis X. McKelvey, *Planning and Design of Airports*, 4th ed. (1993), is a comprehensive civil engineering text on the planning, layout, and design of airports with strong emphasis on aspects such as aircraft pavements and drainage. Christopher R. Blow, *Airport Terminals*, 2nd ed. (1995), provides an architectural view of the functioning of airport passenger terminals with extensive coverage of design case studies.

Norman Ashford, H.P. Martin Stanton, and Clifton A. Moore, *Airport Operations*, 2nd ed. (1996), extensively discusses many aspects of airport operation and management, including administrative structure, security, safety, environmental impact, performance indices, and passenger and aircraft handling. Norman Ashford and Clifton A. Moore, *Airport Finance*, 2nd ed. (1999), discusses the revenue and expenditure patterns of airport authorities, methods of financing, business planning, and project appraisal.

INDEX

A

Abruzzo, Ben L., 28
Ader, Clément, 41–42
Aeroflot, 71–72, 79, 92
aeronautical infrastructure,
    68–69
Airbus, 94
Air Force One, 96–98
airlines, 61–62, 63–64
    the first, 56–60
    postwar, 71–74
    reequipment of, 89–92
airmail, 60–61, 62
airplanes
    aviation pioneers, 36, 38–51
    famous early flights, 53–56
    improvements in technology,
        61–69
    invention of, 36–51
    jet planes, 82–103
    problem of control and, 36,
        46–48
    problem of lift and, 36, 37–40
    problem of propulsion and, 36,
        40–46
    World War II and, 56, 64, 67,
        68, 69–71
airports, 69, 123–144
    airfield lighting, 134
    airport security, 140–144
    air traffic control, 135–136

cargo facilities, 136–138
environmental impact,
    138–140
navigational aids, 133–134
operational requirements, 128
runway configurations, 129–131
runway markings, 134–135
runway pavements, 131–133
airships, 31–35, 65
    types of, 31–32
air traffic control, 135–136
Alcock, John, 53
Allen, Bryan, 120, 121
Amundsen, Roald, 34
Anderson, Maxie, 28
Anderson, Orville, 13
Antonov AN-2, 79
Aoki, Rocky, 28
Arban, Françoise, 11
Archimedes' principle, 2, 4
Artingstall, F.D., 40
autogiros, 76–77, 107, 108
avionics, 98–100

B

Bacon, John M., 11
balloon flight, 1–17, 18–31
    about hot-air balloons, 16–17,
        18–23
    elements of, 2–4
    the first, 1